Galatoire's
COOKBOOK

Galatoire's
COOKBOOK

RECIPES AND FAMILY HISTORY

FROM THE

TIME-HONORED NEW ORLEANS RESTAURANT

To: Todd & Paula
"Best Wishes &
Good Eating!"

Melvin Rodrigue

MELVIN RODRIGUE WITH JYL BENSON

Clarkson Potter/Publishers

New York

Published in the United States by Clarkson Potter/Publishers, an imprint of the Crown Publishing Group,
a division of Random House, Inc., New York.
www.crownpublishing.com
www.clarksonpotter.com

Clarkson N. Potter is a trademark and Potter and colophon are registered trademarks of Random House, Inc.

Library of Congress Cataloging-in-Publication Data
Rodrigue, Melvin.
Galatoire's cookbook : recipes and family history from the time-honored New Orleans restaurant / by Melvin Rodrigue with Jyl Benson. — 1st ed.
Includes index.
1. Cookery, American—Louisiana style.   2. Galatoire's Restaurant.   I. Benson, Jyl.   II. Title.
TX715.2.L68R67   2005
647.95763'35—dc22   2005007532

ISBN 0-307-23637-4

Printed in the United States of America

Design by Maggie Hinders

10   9   8   7   6   5   4   3   2

For the members of the Galatoire family. Today's generation of Galatoires have made

unparalleled efforts to honor previous generations and secure the restaurant's future.

That they have held their family business together for 100 years,

through five generations, is an achievement

of which they should be proud.

Acknowledgments

THIS BOOK would not have been possible without the recollections of some and the talents of others, most notably Chef Ross Eirich. He spent hours helping to create picture-perfect dishes and assisting with recipes. At the same time, he continued to execute the often thankless task of keeping the restaurant running on full steam in concert with David Gooch, Justin Frey, Michele Galatoire, Jacque Fortier, Arnold Chabbaud, Rickey Crochet, Murray Thomas, Emanuel January, Bryant Sylvester, and the rest of the management and staff.

Thanks also to Eugenia Uhl and Louis Sahuc for their sensational photography, and Maggie Hinders and the design team at Clarkson Potter for applying style and insight to the photographic vision and our words to create a sensational finished work. Our cups runneth over for Terri Landry, who painstakingly prepared and tested every single recipe. We would like to thank our agent, Judith Weber of Sobel Weber Associates, for her expert guidance and stellar connections. You cut a sweet deal! We are overwhelmed with gratitude for our editor, Aliza Fogelson. Her patience seems truly inexhaustible, though we did our best to wear her down.

We are grateful to Christian and Sonja Ansel, Simone Nugent, Carolyn and Don Rodman, Leon Touzet, Jr., Leon Touzet, Sr., David Gooch, Clarisse Gooch, Justin Frey, and Michele Galatoire for sharing their family memories and recollections. Kevin McCaffery and Neil Alexander helped us with the laborious interview process, and Erin Barrilleaux did her best to keep us organized. Pomeroy Lowry was generous enough to share her university research paper on Galatoire's. It's our favorite subject, too! We thank Angus Lind of the *Times-Picayune* for allowing us to reprint his very poignant musings on the subject of Galatoire's. Kay McKay Fitzmorris, Laura Claverie, Elizabeth Bowman, and David Woolverton were generous in sharing their personal memories of Galatoire's and we thank you. Thanks to the Mystic Krewe of Barkus: We finally have a Carnival krewe that patronized Galatoire's and no other.

This would not have happened without the influence of Galatoire's sensational family of employees. They come in every day to the daunting task of satisfying every customer who walks through the front door. Our heavily tenured waiters and cooks, bartenders, bussers, porters, hostesses, and office personnel come in daily and do the best job they can in order to make our restaurant the best it can be and maintain our top status in one of America's great food cities.

Last but far from least, thank you to our extended family. Our loyal customer base, which supports us year after year, and generation after generation, is the lifeblood of this establishment.

And finally we would like to praise our respective spouses (Gina Rodrigue and Andrew Fox) and children (Caroline, Savanah, Eugenie, and Adelaide Rodrigue, and Cecilia E. Benson McAlear) for enduring many late nights and weekends alone and countless frantic, screaming, frustrated telephone calls between us. We raise a toast to you all and wish a Happy Birthday to Galatoire's!

MELVIN RODRIGUE AND JYL BENSON
April 2005

Contents

Introduction

WELCOME TO GALATOIRE'S RESTAURANT. Since 1905, legions of long-time regulars have been willing to stand in line for hours on the sidewalk to secure a table. They remain undaunted by the strict "No Reservations" policy for the highly desirable downstairs main dining room. They know that when they finally take their seats, they will be surrounded by familiar faces and their favorite cocktails will already await them. Many of these folks could not even tell you what the menu looks like. They will simply say, "Just bring whatever looks good," to their trusted, courtly waiter, whom they asked for by name when they arrived at the door. Galatoire's waiters are the last of a vanishing breed, for whom serving is both an art and a life calling. At their discretion piquant Shrimp Rémoulade, luscious Crabmeat Canapé Lorenzo, elegant Broiled Pompano with Meunière Butter, silky Veal Liver with Bacon and Onions, or a Fried Soft-shell Crab still sweet with the brine of the sea

might appear before the patrons, whom the waiters refer to as their *préférés*. At Galatoire's one need not speak to have a wish fulfilled. The sight of ice at the bottom of a glass is a well-known cue. Just as sure as the sun will rise, a fresh cocktail—a Sazerac, a Creole Bloody Mary, or, perhaps, a Classic Martini—will appear.

For decades, the tradition of classic fare done simply and without showmanship has been a cornerstone of Galatoire's reputation. Unlike many modern restaurants, Galatoire's cuisine is not the handiwork of a singular superstar chef, but rather of a family that has carefully safeguarded its traditions of quality in the tangible culinary product and the restaurant's intangible image and ambience. Through the ages the recipes that have made the restaurant famous have been passed down orally from cook to cook, many of whom were classically trained French chefs. Others had no idea what culinary school was. They had simply grown up in New Orleans families and learned the secrets of the region's great Creole dishes in the kitchens of their mothers and grandmothers. It is this rich, zesty, amalgamated French Creole heritage that Galatoire's still honors today.

The secrets of these classic dishes will be disclosed in this book. Many of the dishes seem unbelievably simple and easy to prepare. In such cases the success of the dish depends upon the freshness and quality of the raw ingredients and upon the nature of the cooking implements used to prepare them. An old, well-seasoned cast-iron frying pan is worth its weight in gold and will put a gleaming stainless-steel and copper vessel to shame. No honest Creole kitchen is complete without an old black iron skillet.

The classic dishes will be denoted throughout the book with the fleur-de-lis emblem. Many of these dishes have been on the menu since 1905 and a few have slipped in over the years since then. Others, such as Poached Sheepshead with Hollandaise Sauce, have been retired. While delicious, the retired dishes are simply not as popular with today's diners as they once were in the days when Jean Galatoire and his three nephews operated the restaurant. What distinguishes all of the classic dishes is that they have graced Galatoire's everyday menu at some time in its history.

This book also recognizes a new era for Galatoire's, and a collection of new recipes to celebrate that era. While Galatoire's day-to-day menu remains much as it has for the past 100 years, a series of specialty wine-pairing dinners was introduced in 1999. The Summer Wine Dinners, which are hosted monthly from June to September, have allowed the kitchen rare opportunities to break with tradition and show a bit of modern flair, while still remaining true to the essential nature of the French Creole style.

Eighty-six years after Jean Galatoire's death, his legacy, Galatoire's restaurant, is regarded as a special, almost magical place where New Orleanians have been celebrating hallmark occasions for five generations. This stately old restaurant with its buoyantly festive air is infinitely more than a place to enjoy a meal. For countless New Orleans families Galatoire's has shared in the making of

memories that range from the everyday ("I found a *fabulous* new pair of shoes!") to life-defining moments ("Will you marry me?"). Many New Orleanians feel that marking a significant life passage in any other place is simply verboten. For others, having Friday lunch or Sunday brunch or dinner anywhere but Galatoire's is equally unthinkable.

In the spring of 2001, *Washingtonian* magazine was right on the mark when it said: "Galatoire's. Women in floppy hats, men in seersucker suits, politicians pressing the flesh, businessmen who have no intention of going back to the office, a few tourists—all settle in for an afternoon of eating, drinking, talking, and table-hopping that sometimes continues into dinner. The atmosphere is more cocktail party than restaurant lunch."

Cocktail party drama always runs high at Galatoire's—and always has. Playwright Tennessee Williams spent so much time drinking and cavorting here that he garnered his own table and later immortalized the restaurant in his greatest drama, *A Streetcar Named Desire*. People come here to eat and drink far more than they ordinarily would. They visit with friends at nearby tables and they visit with virtual strangers, turning them into afternoon—and even lifelong—friends. In a world that's become too serious, Galatoire's is a place where frivolity rules and adults are given license to leave their cares at the door, act foolish, and have fun. So those who dine here keep coming back. They tell their friends and families about Galatoire's, and then they come, too. The pleasures have continued for 100 years.

Friday lunch is the most popular meal of the week at Galatoire's and many patrons arrive for lunch, order a cocktail, start talking, and simply stay right through dinner. For a collection of New Orleans locals this practice takes on nearly maniacal meaning on both the Friday before Mardi Gras and the Friday before Christmas, the restaurant's busiest days. In order to guarantee tables in the downstairs dining room, determined patrons have established the custom of hiring others to stand in line for them. These "placeholders" often arrive as early as the preceding Tuesday evening, bringing cots, pillows, blankets, radios, card tables, board games, and libations to comfort them during the long wait on the Bourbon Street sidewalk. Sometime around eleven o'clock on Friday morning the patron will arrive and pay his or her placeholder for the place in line. For these patrons it is money well spent. They know the experience they will have will renew and revitalize them. Food will nourish their bodies while exuberance nourishes their spirits.

"Galatoire's is not a restaurant, it's a religion," Galatoire's patron Henri Schindler told *Saveur* magazine in October 1997. "It's a refuge that gives you peace and consolation. It's another world, a place where you can go and know that things will never change."

DEFINING CREOLE CUISINE

New Orleans's exotic culture is largely the result of nearly a century of rule that repeatedly shifted from French to Spanish, tempered by constant large influxes of Anglo-Saxon, Italian, German, Irish, and African immigrants. The city's European heritage is strikingly evident in its architecture, cuisine, and social structure and in the mannerisms of those who call it home.

Like our European brethren, for many New Orleanians, sitting down to the dinner table is a celebrated event, worthy of several hours of one's time. Slowly cooked regional specialties are prepared with the intention that they will be savored at length and deeply appreciated—not gobbled down in a frantic race to get back to everyday life. The people of New Orleans have embraced nourishment with such passion as to garner the motto "We don't eat to live. We live to eat." Nowhere are New Orleans's diverse origins more discernible than in the city's cuisine.

The delicacies found on the New Orleans table have delighted many. Area waters abound with a plenitude of plump blue crabs, salty oysters, several varieties of shrimp, and a bounty of excellent fish. The rich, fertile delta soil pours forth produce and spices. Throughout the region, the French, African, and Spanish culinary traditions of those who settled here absorbed the local bounty and created the beloved cuisines now known as Cajun and Creole.

The elegant, refined Creole cooking style developed by the French and Spanish colonialists is best exemplified by its sauces. This food style has historically been associated with the city and it is more subtle and understated than its bold country cousin. Creole food reveals itself in layers, through a developed range of flavors from ample spices and aromatics, whereas Cajun food's flavor is imparted by robust peppery flavors and smoked meats.

At Galatoire's we celebrate the Creole culinary style and its heritage while remaining true to our French roots. Thus we have coined the term "French Creole" cuisine.

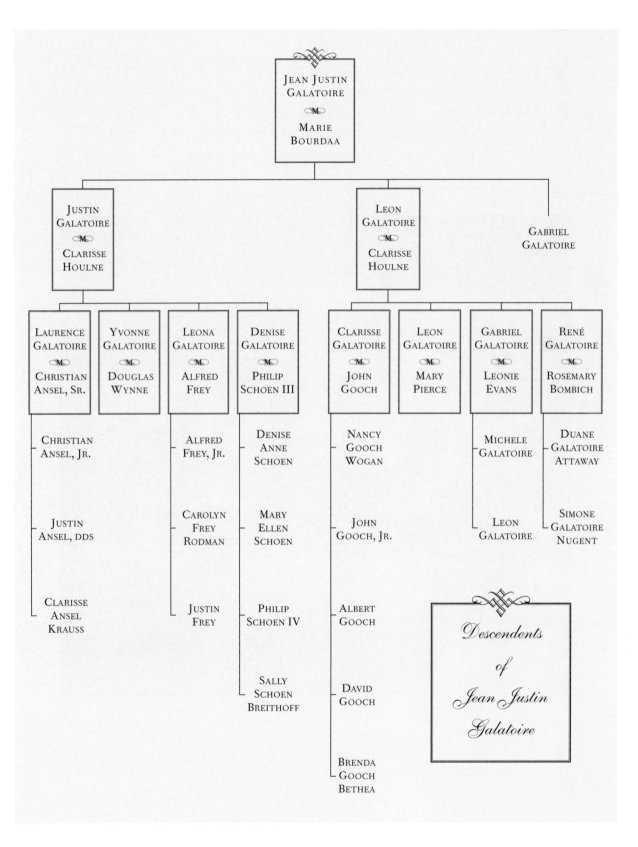

JEAN JUSTIN
GALATOIRE
M
MARIE
BOURDAA

JUSTIN
GALATOIRE
M
CLARISSE
HOULNE

LEON
GALATOIRE
M
CLARISSE
HOULNE

GABRIEL
GALATOIRE

LAURENCE
GALATOIRE
M
CHRISTIAN
ANSEL, SR.

YVONNE
GALATOIRE
M
DOUGLAS
WYNNE

LEONA
GALATOIRE
M
ALFRED
FREY

DENISE
GALATOIRE
M
PHILIP
SCHOEN III

CLARISSE
GALATOIRE
M
JOHN
GOOCH

LEON
GALATOIRE
M
MARY
PIERCE

GABRIEL
GALATOIRE
M
LEONIE
EVANS

RENÉ
GALATOIRE
M
ROSEMARY
BOMBICH

CHRISTIAN
ANSEL, JR.

ALFRED
FREY, JR.

DENISE
ANNE
SCHOEN

NANCY
GOOCH
WOGAN

MICHELE
GALATOIRE

DUANE
GALATOIRE
ATTAWAY

JUSTIN
ANSEL, DDS

CAROLYN
FREY
RODMAN

MARY
ELLEN
SCHOEN

JOHN
GOOCH, JR.

LEON
GALATOIRE

SIMONE
GALATOIRE
NUGENT

CLARISSE
ANSEL
KRAUSS

JUSTIN
FREY

PHILIP
SCHOEN IV

ALBERT
GOOCH

SALLY
SCHOEN
BREITHOFF

DAVID
GOOCH

*Descendents
of
Jean Justin
Galatoire*

BRENDA
GOOCH
BETHEA

THE GALATOIRE FAMILY

New Orleans gourmands responded enthusiastically when Jean Galatoire opened the doors to his namesake restaurant on Bourbon Street in the city's French Quarter in 1905. The gracious dining experience Jean offered was inspired by the dining style of his hometown, Pardies, a small village near Pau, France, an elegant, picturesque city in the foothills of the Pyrénées Mountains. In this region meals were lengthy, relaxed, and bountiful, and wine and spirits flowed for hours and hours alongside easy conversation.

"His recipe for success probably came right from his mother's table," said Leon Touzet, Jr., a great-great-nephew of Jean. "The formula at Galatoire's was simple and it is the same today as it was then: copious portions of excellent food; very potent, generous cocktails; and great service. Eating at Galatoire's is more like eating in the comfortable home of a special friend. The only difference is that this friend never runs out of food and drink. No one is in any hurry to leave."

Jean was an energetic man who had an instinct for fine foods and pleasurable dining. When he departed from Pardies in 1874, he carried with him the recipes and traditions of his native culture. He and his wife, Gabrielle Marchal Galatoire, first settled in Birmingham, Alabama, then in Chicago, and finally arrived in New Orleans around 1900. Jean opened a bar near the Louisville & Nashville (L & N) train station at the foot of Canal Street. When his brother, Jean Justin, died unexpectedly in Pardies and left behind his widow, Marie Bourdaa, and their seven children, Jean agreed that Marie should send some of her sons to New Orleans, where he could put them to work and lighten her heavy burden. The first of Jean's nephews to take up the offer was fifteen-year-old Justin. In 1902 this brave young boy arrived in New Orleans. Uncle Jean quickly put young Justin to work at the bar and paid him twenty-five cents a day for hours on end of arduous labor. Many years later Justin recalled his mother's correspondence with his uncle Jean, saying, "My

ABOVE: *Jean Galatoire, founder of Galatoire's, 1854–1919.* RIGHT, CLOCKWISE FROM TOP: *Marie, Justin, Madeleine, Irenee, Leon, Eugene, and Amelie Galatoire.*

mother wrote to see if he did not have work for us . . . and he had work, yes. Thirteen, fourteen hours a day!"

Not long after Jean sold the bar near the L & N station, he purchased Victor Bero's eponymous eatery, Victor's, which had been established in the mid-1800s. One hundred years ago, when Jean assumed the role of restaurateur, his first action was to remove the hams and game that hung from ropes in the restaurant's front windows. He appointed his wife cashier, put young Justin to work, and changed the name above the door to "Galatoire's."

Jean Galatoire crafted the menu in his new eatery from a combination of traditional French dishes, many of which had been handed down through generations, and favorite holdovers from Victor's menu.

In 1911, Jean purchased from Marie Odile Carr the lovely 1830s three-story brick Creole town house in which the restaurant is still housed. Though the French Quarter property is worth millions today, Jean picked it up for a thrifty twenty-five thousand dollars. At the time of Jean's purchase the townhouse was sandwiched between Randon's Cleaners and Madame Rapho's, a ladies' shop specializing in fine linens and gowns. Today the restaurant's immediate neighbors include a shop specializing in "adult" items, strip clubs catering to a myriad of tastes, touristy T-shirt and knickknack shops, and bars that thump with blaring music at all hours.

ABOVE: *Galatoire's Restaurant, circa 1905.*
LEFT: *The New Orleans Men's Coffee Association's first banquet was held in the private room on the second floor of Galatoire's in 1913.*

Galatoire's has become a bastion of civilization on an otherwise bawdy block. That elegantly dressed upscale locals will consistently brave the melee and stand outside in line for a table is a revealing testament to their devotion to Galatoire's and the delights that lie within.

Justin's older brother, Leon, immigrated to the United States in 1906 at the age of twenty-two, most likely after finishing an apprenticeship in France in the Galatoire family's traditional livelihood as *marchands de cochon* (pork merchants). Leon worked for a time at the Cosmopolitan

Restaurant on Bourbon Street before joining Justin in the employ of their uncle. The trio of brothers was complete when the youngest, Gabriel, age twenty, arrived in the city in 1912. The three poured their collective efforts and talents into the daily rigors of running one of New Orleans's most popular eateries. While the brothers shared a strong work ethic and a drive to succeed, the differences in their personalities lent themselves well to the unique demands of the restaurant. Justin, a natural leader, was friendly, diplomatic, personable, and service-oriented. He slipped easily into the role of manager. Leon, though older, was more reserved and preferred to arrive early in the morning, between five and six o'clock, to tend to deliveries, inventory, and bookkeeping. Playful, gregarious Gabriel either greeted guests at the door or interacted with them from the restau-

rant's signature carved desk at the rear of the main dining room. His ebullient nature set patrons at ease and he encouraged them to eat and drink heartily and enjoy themselves.

In 1919, his health failing, Jean sold Galatoire's to his three nephews for forty thousand dollars. He died later that year at the age of sixty-five.

The third generation of Galatoires joined the family business soon after. In 1922, upon completing an apprenticeship as a cook in Pau, Leon Touzet, Sr., set sail for the United States on the *Rochambeau* with his uncle Gabriel, who had returned to France for a visit and to fetch his young nephew for a new life in America. The three brothers immediately put

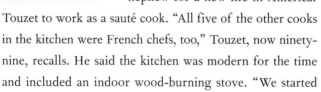

Touzet to work as a sauté cook. "All five of the other cooks in the kitchen were French chefs, too," Touzet, now ninety-nine, recalls. He said the kitchen was modern for the time and included an indoor wood-burning stove. "We started

The second generation of Galatoires, who bought the restaurant from founder Jean (clockwise from top): Justin, Gabriel, and Leon Galatoire.

work at six o'clock in the morning and at seven or eight o'clock a tray of pony glasses filled with Chartreuse, cognac, or marc would be passed for all of us to enjoy. It was customary for us to begin our day this way in the kitchen."

A relentless work schedule, absolutely grueling by today's standards, was also customary. "Uncle Justin made everyone work seven days a week, twelve hours a day," Touzet said. "If you wanted time off you had to pay someone else to work for you."

The restaurant opened at eleven a.m. for lunch, and nattily dressed businessmen dined on the *plats du jour* (daily specials). These hearty meals included courses of soup, fish, meat, vegetables, and dessert. Offerings included both Creole selections and homey French classics such as trout meunière, roast leg of lamb with flageolets, trout marguery, and the like.

The *plat du jour* was discontinued in the 1940s during World War II, when government rations on produce made it impossible to maintain. At Gabriel's suggestion, the menu became the extensive à la carte book that it is today.

World War II also brought an end to the era of Galatoire's *chambres privées* (private dining rooms) on the second floor. With a knowing look, Leon Touzet, Sr., acknowledges that most private parties were private parties of two, and both staff members and other patrons made a sport of speculating as to what was going on up there behind the closed doors.

In a 1956 article for *Holiday* magazine, Shirley Ann Grau wrote: "Galatoire's was a favorite rendezvous. The social structure of New Orleans was quite rigid, and until the twenties it was not considered proper for a single woman to appear in a restaurant with anyone but relatives. Private rooms were the answer. The separate entrance assured privacy and the waiters were discreet."

Because of the military draft there was a shortage of men available to keep both floors staffed.

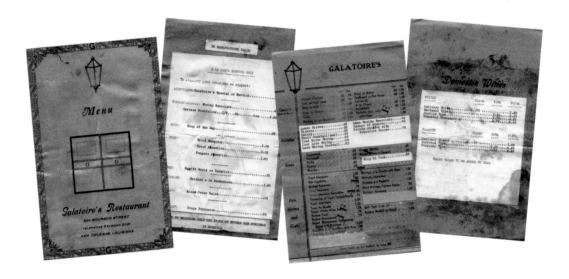

Additionally, most household budgets had been redirected toward basic necessities instead of fun and frivolity. The time had come to close the second floor and do away with the much-discussed *chambres privées*. The second floor was shuttered and used only for storage and office space until many years later.

While Gabriel never married, Justin and Leon married first cousins, both of whom bore the name Clarisse Houlne. Justin had four daughters: Laurence, Yvonne, Leona, and Denise. Leon fathered one daughter and three sons: Clarisse, Leon, Gabriel, and René. Both men strove to keep their family lives separate from their work at the restaurant. Carolyn Rodman, granddaughter of Justin, said it is entirely possible that her grandmother may never even have dined at the restaurant. Instead the families would gather every Sunday for a big dinner at one of the two brothers' French Quarter homes.

Justin's daughter Yvonne Galatoire Wynne ("My father's son by default," she said) was called in to work at the family restaurant one day in 1938 when the regular cashier took ill. The cashier died and Miss Yvonne remained at her new post beneath the restaurant's familiar clock. She became a much-beloved personality at Galatoire's. She was a manager from 1964 until she retired in 1997. She was also president of the business from 1984 until she died in 2000.

Yvonne, an egalitarian in the same vein as her father, was known to treat everyone, rich or poor, with the same degree of respect. She staunchly upheld the "No Reservations" policy that was initiated by her great-uncle Jean. He had felt that everyone deserved the same chance of enjoying a meal at his restaurant and he was amazed by the competitiveness that had erupted over just that. "This is just a little chicken place," he told his family. "What's the big deal?"

ABOVE: *The fifty-year celebration of Justin Galatoire.* LEFT: *Yvonne Galatoire Wynne.* OPPOSITE: *Menu from World War II, when food was rationed.*

"Everyone calls up saying he has a big shot in town he wants to entertain," Yvonne told *The States Item* in June 1972. "It's always big shots."

With Yvonne stationed at the cashier's desk, Leon and Justin continued to manage Galatoire's together after Gabriel's death in 1945. Justin remained the lone second-generation member of the restaurant's management team when Leon retired in 1961. By that time other members of the third generation had followed Yvonne's lead and joined the family business.

When Laurence Galatoire married Christian Ansel, the family was so pleased that they invited him to join the business. He served in a managerial position from 1947 until his sudden death in 1964. Also on staff were two sons of Leon, René and Gabriel (known as "Gabie"), both of whom had served in World War II.

Gabie was charming and debonair. He worked the front of the house and was known to greet customers at the door and direct them to their seats with football terminology, instructing them to sit on a particular "yard line" or "between the goal posts."

René is fondly remembered for his genuine humility and frequent acts of kindness. When he returned from the war to take his place in the family business he brought with him the honors and distinctions of a Purple Heart and a Bronze Star for having sustained injuries while saving the life of another soldier. He began his restaurant career in Galatoire's kitchen and later moved to the dining room as general manager. René became president of the company in 1973 when his uncle Justin died at the age of eighty-seven, and René retained that position until he retired in 1984.

Justin's grandson Christian Ansel, Jr., returned from Paris, where he was working as an engineer, to take his place in the family business after the unexpected death of his father. He remained on staff from 1966 until 1973, when he left to establish Christian's, another critically acclaimed, award-winning New Orleans restaurant. He retired in 1996

ABOVE, CLOCKWISE FROM TOP: *Chris Ansel, Sr.; a waiter at Galatoire's confers with Yvonne Wynne; René Galatoire.*
OPPOSITE, CLOCKWISE FROM TOP: *Gabriel "Gabie" Galatoire, René Galatoire; Justin Frey; Michele Galatoire; David Gooch.*

and continues to serve on Galatoire's board of directors.

Other fourth-generation members of the Galatoire family continue to own and operate the restaurant today. Justin Frey, Justin Galatoire's grandson; Michele Galatoire, Leon Galatoire's granddaughter; and David Gooch, Leon Galatoire's grandson, are involved in its daily management. Another of Leon's grandsons, who also bears his name, served in the family business for nearly twenty years.

A comprehensive physical restoration of the building, including the second floor, was completed in 1999. In order for Galatoire's to remain competitive, it was time to make a few subtle changes. When it reopened for business after the renovations Galatoire's began to accept reservations for the new upstairs dining rooms, which also accommodate private parties. A patron bar gave those awaiting tables for the downstairs dining room (for which reservations are still not accepted) a place to gather other than the Bourbon Street sidewalk beyond the door.

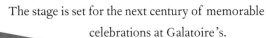

In the years to come, stewardship of Galatoire's restaurant will pass into the hands of the fifth generation of Jean's family. Though the food at Galatoire's is, indeed, sublime, the restaurant's century of continued success and its certain success in the future must be ascribed to the close-knit Galatoire family. It is their continued embrace of their heritage and devotion to Jean's initial vision; their relationships with one another, their devoted staff, and the New Orleans community that have imbued their family business with a life of its own.

The stage is set for the next century of memorable celebrations at Galatoire's.

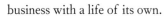

Cocktails

WITH THE BLESSING of King Louis XIV of France, two French-Canadian brothers, Pierre Le Moyne, Sieur d'Iberville, and Jean-Baptiste Le Moyne, Sieur de Bienville, set sail from France in 1698 with shiploads of alcoholic libations and liquor-laden treats. They departed with the intention of establishing a colony at the mouth of the Mississippi River. To be without their creature comforts was simply unthinkable. In 1699, they unpacked their larders at the mouth of the Mississippi and set to the business of effectively establishing a society with a penchant for wine and spirits. These passions are very much alive today.

In European fashion, it was unusual, even rude, for an early New Orleans host to fail to offer guests some type of apéritif just as soon as they walked in the door. If guests were to stay for dinner it was expected that a different wine would accompany each course, as many as seven in all.

Large social gatherings, such as soirées or Carnival balls, brought with them numerous potent concoctions in the form of punches, toddies, cordials, crèmes, and brews in addition to the traditional wines and liqueurs.

Is it any wonder that New Orleans is the home of the cocktail?

Antoine Peychaud, an apothecary, arrived in town in 1793. His son, also named Antoine, began dispensing a "tonic" to his clients from his shop on Toulouse Street. The quick fix to aches, pains, and aggravation was a mixture of brandy and a secret formula Peychaud called "bitters." He served the mixture around 1838 in a double-ended egg cup known in French as a *coquetier*. Most Americans wrecked the pronunciation; perhaps this came about after too many *coquetiers*. In any event, out came something that sounded like "cocktail." And it stuck.

New Orleanians, therefore, own the cocktail. We love our spirits.

On the quality of Galatoire's cocktails, Chris Ansel, Jr., recalls, "My grandfather Justin Galatoire always said, 'The first thing the customer sees is his drink. If the drink is not up to par, then the customer will find fault with everything. But if you give him a good drink when he first sits down, he will order another one.'"

CREOLE BLOODY MARY

Bloody Marys are very popular at Galatoire's, usually as a starter cocktail to kick off lunch or weekend brunch. It is customary for members of the waitstaff to bring their patrons dishes of accoutrements for embellishing and flavoring their Bloody Marys. So generous are the plates of tiny pickled Gibson onions, spiced green beans, olives, and sometimes celery and pickled okra that they serve almost as salads.

1½ OUNCES PREMIUM VODKA

2 OR 3 DROPS OF TABASCO SAUCE

3 OUNCES TOMATO JUICE

SALT AND FRESHLY GROUND BLACK PEPPER TO TASTE

FRESH LEMON JUICE TO TASTE

½ TEASPOON WORCESTERSHIRE SAUCE

ICE

TINY PICKLED ONIONS, LIME WEDGES, CELERY STALKS,
    SPICY PICKLED GREEN BEANS, AND/OR GREEN
    OLIVES, FOR GARNISH, IF DESIRED

Shake the vodka, Tabasco, tomato juice, salt, pepper, lemon juice, Worcestershire and ice in a cocktail shaker. Strain and serve over ice. Serve with garnish of your choice.

MAKES 1 COCKTAIL

BRANDY OR BOURBON MILK PUNCH

This frothy starter is wildly popular with the weekend brunch crowd. It is rich and sweet and usually serves as a prelude to champagne.

---

2 OUNCES PREMIUM BRANDY OR BOURBON

5 OUNCES WHOLE MILK

½ TEASPOON VANILLA EXTRACT

1 TEASPOON SIMPLE SYRUP (PAGE 35)

ICE

1 DASH OF NUTMEG

Pour the brandy or bourbon, milk, vanilla, and simple syrup into a cocktail shaker. Fill a highball glass to almost full with ice cubes, and transfer the ice to the shaker. Shake well and pour the drink into the highball glass. Dust the top of the drink with nutmeg.

MAKES 1 COCKTAIL

CHAMPAGNE COCKTAIL

Young ladies particularly enjoy this apéritif.

1 DASH OF PEYCHAUD'S BITTERS

1 SUGAR CUBE

5 OUNCES CHILLED CHAMPAGNE

1 LEMON TWIST

Dash the bitters directly onto the sugar cube. Drop the cube into the bottom of a champagne flute, and then fill the glass with the chilled champagne. Garnish with a lemon twist.

MAKES 1 COCKTAIL

CLASSIC MARTINI

This is our most popular cocktail. Straight chilled vodka or gin, no vermouth or other distractions. Garnish if you must.

1½ OUNCES PREMIUM GIN OR VODKA

ICE

OLIVES, COCKTAIL ONIONS, OR LEMON OR LIME TWIST, FOR GARNISH, IF DESIRED

Stir the vodka or gin with ice. Strain and serve either on the rocks or in a chilled cocktail glass. Garnish as desired.

MAKES 1 COCKTAIL

SAZERAC COCKTAIL

The name of this unusual cocktail stems from the Sazerac Coffee House in New Orleans, where the drink was allegedly first created. The intoxicating beverage was originally made with Sazerac-du-Forge, a French brandy, which was later replaced with rye whiskey, and with Peychaud's bitters.

2 OR 3 DROPS OF HERBSAINT OR PERNOD LIQUEUR	1 DASH OF PEYCHAUD'S BITTERS
ICE	2 TEASPOONS SIMPLE SYRUP (PAGE 35)
2 OUNCES PREMIUM RYE WHISKEY	1 LEMON TWIST

Coat the inside of a rocks glass with the Herbsaint. Add ice to the glass, then pour in the rye whiskey and add the bitters and simple syrup. Garnish with a lemon twist.

MAKES 1 COCKTAIL

GALATOIRE'S SPECIAL COCKTAIL

This cocktail is similar to the famous Sazerac cocktail, only it utilizes bourbon instead of rye whiskey.

2 OR 3 DROPS OF HERBSAINT OR PERNOD LIQUEUR	1 DASH OF PEYCHAUD'S BITTERS
ICE	2 TEASPOONS SIMPLE SYRUP (PAGE 35)
2 OUNCES PREMIUM BOURBON	1 LEMON TWIST

Coat the inside of a rocks glass with the Herbsaint. Add ice to the glass, then pour in the bourbon and add the bitters and simple syrup. Garnish with a lemon twist.

MAKES 1 COCKTAIL

OLD-FASHIONED

A sweet and potent southern favorite, this cocktail has been stylish and anything but "old-fashioned" since it was initially concocted in the late 1880s.

ICE

2 OUNCES PREMIUM BOURBON OR OTHER WHISKEY

1 DASH OF PEYCHAUD'S BITTERS

2 TEASPOONS SIMPLE SYRUP (PAGE 35)

1 SLICE OF ORANGE

1 MARASCHINO CHERRY

Fill a rocks glass with ice and add the bourbon or whiskey, bitters, and simple syrup. Garnish with an orange slice and cherry.

MAKES 1 COCKTAIL

OJEN COCKTAIL

CRUSHED ICE

3 OUNCES OJEN LIQUEUR

2 DASHES OF PEYCHAUD'S BITTERS

Fill a rocks glass with crushed ice. Pour the liqueur over the ice. Dash the bitters over the liqueur and allow it to permeate the drink before serving.

MAKES 1 COCKTAIL

SIMPLE SYRUP

A necessity at every well-stocked bar. This will keep for two months when stored in an airtight container.

1 CUP WATER   1 ½ CUPS SUGAR

Add the water to a small pot set over high heat and bring it to a boil. Place the sugar in a small mixing bowl. Remove the water from the stove and carefully pour it into the bowl with the sugar. Whisk the mixture continuously until the sugar is dissolved. Allow the syrup to cool. It will appear cloudy at first but will clear as it cools.

MAKES 1 ½ CUPS

Traditions bind our society, our faiths, our families and friends. Many of us find it reassuring to know how we will share significant occasions with those most important to us, where we will gather, what we will eat, who will be there (and often, what they will say, do, and wear).

"Traditions are wonderful," said Kay McKay Fitzmorris. "They create memories that sustain and comfort us; they remind us of the joy and laughter we shared through the years as a family."

Celebrating New Year's Eve as a family tradition began for the McKay family more than forty years ago. Kay Fitzmorris's parents, Jim and Kitty McKay, would rush home from friends' parties to be with their seven children for the bells ringing in the New Year. "As we got older we began the wonderful tradition of going to lunch on New Year's Eve," Fitzmorris said. "Through the years, as each of us married, our spouses joined our family in these memorable celebrations.

"We reminisced over the year, gave toasts, sang, laughed, and sometimes cried," Fitzmorris said. "It seemed as if we saved all the exciting, significant news to announce at our luncheon."

When Jim and Kitty McKay died, their family found comfort in continuing the New Year's Eve luncheon tradition.

On New Year's Eve 1999, Galatoire's became a part of that tradition. It had always been a favorite restaurant for the family, but the "no reservations" policy made it impossible for such a large gathering. When the restaurant reopened the upstairs dining room and began accepting reservations, Galatoire's became a natural choice.

"Last year our sister Mikie (Stackpole), ill with terminal cancer, celebrated her last New Year's Eve with us. We were at Galatoire's. It was her favorite restaurant," Fitzmorris said. "We shared the upstairs dining room that day with our dear friends, the LeBlanc family. It was so much fun!"

And another family's new tradition was born that day.

"For a number of years now I have admired the McKay family's New Year's Eve tradition," said Adrianne LeBlanc. "When I heard Galatoire's was taking reservations, I decided to make one months in advance with the hope that all could join us. I didn't really tell anyone about the reservation until closer to the date. I just told them to mark their calendars."

"We enjoyed the most wonderful time," Mrs. LeBlanc said.

The twenty-seven members of the LeBlanc family and fifteen McKays have returned to Galatoire's for New Year's Eve every year since.

The huge group arrives for the first seating in order to enjoy the entire afternoon together.

There is never a dull moment.

"Because my oldest brother is a Jesuit priest and the McKays' oldest brother is an appeals court judge, religion and politics are safe topics for dinner conversation," Mrs. LeBlanc said. Everyone has his or her favorite waiters. Dorris, Bryant, Johnny, and Louis add to the party-like atmosphere.

"We love the food!" Mrs. LeBlanc said. "We begin with an array of appetizers and move to a variety of entrées to share. The Trout Meunière and stuffed eggplant are probably the two favorites."

Above all, the families cherish being together.

"Galatoire's takes our celebration and creates magic," Mrs. LeBlanc said.

"For that time, in that place, we are all young again, all carefree, all happy to be together," Mrs. Fitzmorris said. "We look forward to many years of dining as a family at Galatoire's."

Hors d'Oeuvres

Whether hand-passed for a formal gathering or simply presented on the kitchen countertop before a backyard barbecue, hors d'oeuvres are an established part of entertaining in New Orleans. They are usually one- or two-bite-size, hot or cold, and might come in the form of an elegant canapé or a simple selection of spreads and crackers. Guests have come to *eat*, not to *wait* to eat!

We drew the hors d'oeuvres selections here from our everyday appetizer menu as well as from special menus created for private parties. They are suggested here as small tastes for a number of guests. However, they would work equally well as seated appetizers and some of them are featured on our everyday menu as such. One example is the luscious Crabmeat Canapé Lorenzo, a favorite dish that many staff members associate with a dearly beloved former patron, Mrs. Marian Atkinson.

Marian Patton Atkinson, a proud cousin of General George Patton, dined at Galatoire's from 1916 until her death in 2000 at the age of ninety-eight. So that she need never wait for Table Ten, her preferred spot, Mrs. Atkinson's private limousine arrived at the curb outside Galatoire's at five p.m. six days a week (except Monday, when the restaurant is closed) for more than thirty years. Upon her arrival the elegant lady would be presented with the first of the two Old-Fashioned cocktails she enjoyed with her evening meal. Her repast typically included three or four courses of house specialties, which very frequently began with the Crabmeat Canapé Lorenzo. Her meal usually lasted about three hours, during which she would hold court from her table as she visited with her fellow patrons.

"Visiting" is one of the most pleasurable aspects associated with hand-passed hors d'oeuvres. Many New Orleanians enjoy cocktails or apéritifs before meals. Hand-passing hors d'oeuvres as accompaniments allows guests the opportunity to mingle and get to know one another before sitting down to a formal meal. At Galatoire's we always begin our specialty dinners with cocktails and hors d'oeuvres at the bar. Most of our private parties begin in this fashion, as well.

When entertaining at home, complete as much of your hors d'oeuvres preparation as possible in advance and keep the beginning of your evening relaxed by offering one signature beverage to set the tone for the gathering. "Visiting" is simply impossible if you are relegated to the kitchen while everyone else mingles and has fun.

SOUFFLÉ POTATOES (*POMMES SOUFFLÉS*)

To many this dish defies logic, and it is always amusing to witness a first encounter with pommes soufflés, *which are literally fried wafers of potato puffed with air.*

This is a simple dish, though mastering the cooking technique will take a bit of effort. Practice on your own before serving this to guests. Their reactions will be well worth the effort. Béarnaise sauce is the perfect accompaniment.

1 GALLON VEGETABLE OIL	SALT TO TASTE
6 IDAHO POTATOES, SCRUBBED	1 RECIPE BÉARNAISE SAUCE (PAGE 250)

In a large, heavy-bottomed pot suitable for frying, heat the oil to 325°F. While the oil heats, slice the potatoes lengthwise ⅛ inch thick using a mandoline or very sharp knife. Trim the square corners from either end of the strips of potato. The result will be a long oval shape.

Place the potatoes into the oil, not more than two layers at a time. Overloading the pot will cause the temperature to drop. In order to maintain a consistent temperature, move the potatoes constantly with a slotted spoon. Cook the potatoes for 4 to 5 minutes, until light brown. Some will form small air bubbles. This is an indication that the meat of the potato has cooked away. Once the potatoes have become inflated, remove them from the hot oil and set aside to cool until just prior to serving.

To prepare this dish in advance, cook the potatoes until they puff, and immediately remove them from the 325°F oil and lay flat on a sheet pan. Place wax paper between the layers of potatoes.

When you are ready to serve the potatoes, increase (or reheat) the temperature of the oil to 375°F. Place the potatoes back into the oil and they will puff instantly. Cook for an additional 30 seconds, stirring continuously until they are golden brown on both sides and crispy enough to hold their form without deflating. Remove the potatoes from the oil and drain them on paper towels. Sprinkle with a pinch of salt while hot. Repeat with remaining potatoes. Serve immediately with béarnaise sauce.

SERVES 10 TO 12

CREOLE FRIED EGGPLANT

For an elegant hors d'oeuvre presentation, line a silver tray with a linen napkin and stack the eggplant batons carefully atop. Offer your guests dishes of béarnaise sauce and confectioners' sugar as accompaniments. Outside of New Orleans you are certain to get odd looks.

Serving fried eggplant with powdered sugar is an old Creole practice that was once employed to mask the bitterness of the vegetable. While bitterness is no longer an issue, many still enjoy the unexpected sweet–savory combination. When serving this dish as an appetizer or side dish, many Galatoire's waiters create, at tableside, a pasty sauce of Tabasco and confectioners' sugar for their guests to enjoy with their eggplant. It's an acquired taste.

---

1 GALLON VEGETABLE OIL

2 LARGE EGGPLANTS, PEELED

2 CUPS ALL-PURPOSE FLOUR

SALT AND FRESHLY GROUND BLACK PEPPER TO TASTE

2 LARGE EGGS

2 CUPS WHOLE MILK

2 CUPS SEASONED DRIED BREAD CRUMBS

1 RECIPE BÉARNAISE SAUCE (PAGE 250)

CONFECTIONERS' SUGAR, FOR SERVING

Heat the oil to 350°F in a heavy pot.

Cut off the rounded ends of the eggplants and discard. Peel the eggplants, then stand each on end and slice lengthwise. Slice each piece lengthwise again to form batons that are approximately ½ × ½ × 6 inches long. To a large mixing bowl add the flour and season it with salt and pepper. Add the eggplant batons and toss to coat. Remove them from the flour, shake off excess, and set aside.

In a separate large mixing bowl, whisk the eggs and milk together. Pass each eggplant baton through the egg wash (it is important to coat each one thoroughly). Add the bread crumbs to a plate or shallow baking pan and roll the batons in the bread crumbs.

Carefully add the eggplant to the hot oil. The eggplant pieces will float to the surface. Use a utensil to keep the batons fully submerged so they will brown evenly, about 5 minutes. Remove the eggplant to drain on a pan that has been double lined with paper towels. Pat gently to remove excess oil. Serve immediately, offering separate dishes of béarnaise sauce and confectioners' sugar as accompaniments.

SERVES 6

SENATOR J. BENNETT JOHNSTON: TAKE YOUR PLACE IN LINE

One famous story depicts retired U.S. Senator J. Bennett Johnston waiting in line on the sidewalk outside of Galatoire's for a table. While Senator Johnston was waiting, President Ronald Reagan placed a call to the senator at the restaurant. The senator walked to the front of the line and entered to take the call. After the two completed their telephone conversation, Senator Johnston graciously returned to his position in line and waited for his turn to be seated. Senator Johnston knew that the tradition of "first come, first served" applied to all customers.

SMOKED SALMON MOUSSE CANAPÉS

Elegant canapés are a favorite of the southern hostess—and a favorite at Galatoire's private parties, when the evening's host would like something light during the cocktail hour. The assertive flavors are perfectly complemented by a glass of cold, crisp pinot grigio or champagne.

For ease when entertaining, the cooled bread rounds and the mousse can be made the day before and stored in separate sealed containers. Refrigerate the mousse. Assemble the canapés just before your guests arrive.

ONE 16-INCH FRENCH BAGUETTE, SLICED INTO ¼-INCH ROUNDS

½ CUP CLARIFIED BUTTER (PAGE 248)

1 BUNCH OF FRESH DILL, STEMS REMOVED

1 POUND SLICED COLD-SMOKED SALMON

8 OUNCES CREAM CHEESE, SOFTENED

2 LARGE EGG YOLKS

¼ CUP CHAMPAGNE OR SPARKLING WINE

¼ CUP FINELY CHOPPED RED ONION

¼ CUP NONPAREIL CAPERS, DRAINED

3 HARD-BOILED EGGS, PEELED AND FINELY CHOPPED

Preheat the oven to 250°F. Brush the bread rounds with clarified butter and bake on a cookie sheet for 10 minutes, or until golden brown and crispy. Just prior to removing the bread rounds from the oven, about 1 minute, finely chop the dill and sprinkle half over the canapés. Reserve the remainder.

Place half of the smoked salmon in a food processor with the cream cheese and egg yolks. Turn on the processor. Process until smooth, using a rubber spatula to scrape the sides of the bowl several times to ensure a uniform consistency. With the machine still running, add the champagne and process briefly, just until the mixture is fluffy. Remove the mousse to a mixing bowl and gently fold in the red onions, capers, and hard-boiled eggs.

Trim the remaining salmon into 1-inch pieces and place them atop the canapés. Using a pastry bag, pipe about 1 tablespoon of mousse atop the salmon and garnish with the remaining chopped dill.

MAKES 60 CANAPÉS

CRABMEAT CANAPÉ LORENZO

The utter beauty of this dish lies in its simplicity: Giant lumps of sweet, succulent white crabmeat are lightly bound together and cooked in a manner that shrouds them in a light, flavorful puff. The final addition of anchovy just prior to broiling allows the pungent flavor to infuse the crab.

4 SLICES WHITE BREAD, TOASTED

¼ CUP CLARIFIED BUTTER (PAGE 248)

½ CUP CHOPPED SCALLIONS (WHITE AND GREEN PARTS)

¼ CUP FINELY CHOPPED CURLY PARSLEY

1 POUND JUMBO LUMP CRABMEAT, CLEANED

SALT AND FRESHLY GROUND WHITE PEPPER TO TASTE

CAYENNE PEPPER TO TASTE

1 CUP BÉCHAMEL SAUCE (PAGE 251)

4 EGG YOLKS

½ CUP SEASONED DRIED BREAD CRUMBS

2 TABLESPOONS GRATED PARMESAN CHEESE

8 ANCHOVY FILLETS

Using a large round cookie cutter or an inverted glass, cut 4-inch circles from the centers of the toasted bread slices. Reserve the circles and discard the bread trimmings. Set aside.

In a large sauté pan, heat 2 tablespoons of the clarified butter over medium-high heat and sauté the scallions and parsley for 3 minutes, or until tender. Gently fold in the crabmeat and continue to sauté until it is heated through. Season with the salt, white pepper, and cayenne pepper. Fold in the béchamel sauce and cook for 4 to 5 minutes, until the mixture just begins to simmer. With a rubber spatula, gently fold in the egg yolks, ¼ cup of the bread crumbs, and 1 tablespoon of the Parmesan cheese. Continue to stir gently over low heat for 1 minute. Remove the pan from the heat and allow the mixture to rest for 2 minutes.

Preheat the broiler. Divide the mixture into 4 equal portions and form into balls. Place each of the balls on a toast circle and compress gently. Crisscross 2 anchovies across the top of each canapé. Mix the remaining ¼ cup bread crumbs and 1 tablespoon Parmesan cheese and sprinkle the canapés evenly with the mixture. Drizzle with the remaining 2 tablespoons clarified butter and place under a broiler until golden brown. Serve immediately.

MAKES 4 CANAPÉS

FRIED OYSTER ROCKEFELLER CANAPÉS WITH HOLLANDAISE

Several components from Galatoire's classic repertoire are brought together in this rich, modern starter.

ONE 12-INCH FRENCH baguette, SLICED INTO ¼-INCH ROUNDS

½ CUP CLARIFIED BUTTER (PAGE 248)

1 CUP ROCKEFELLER SAUCE (SEE PAGE 74)

1 GALLON VEGETABLE OIL

2 CUPS YELLOW CORN FLOUR (MUCH FINER THAN CORN MEAL)

1 TEASPOON SALT

1 TEASPOON FRESHLY GROUND BLACK PEPPER

2 DOZEN LARGE LOUISIANA OYSTERS

1 CUP HOLLANDAISE SAUCE (PAGE 249)

Preheat the oven to 250°F. Brush the bread rounds with the clarified butter and bake for 10 minutes, or until golden brown and crispy. Spread the Rockefeller sauce evenly atop the canapés, taking care to cover the entire surface. The edges will burn under the broiler if they are not sauced. Set aside.

Heat the oil to 350°F in a large, heavy-bottomed pot suitable for frying.

Combine the corn flour, salt, and pepper in a mixing bowl. Dredge the oysters in the seasoned corn flour, shaking to remove excess flour. Fry the oysters for 3 to 4 minutes, or until they float to the surface and turn golden brown. Do not overcook. Remove them with a slotted spoon and drain atop a platter lined with paper towels.

Preheat the broiler. Place the sauce-covered canapés under the broiler. Watch closely and remove the canapés as soon as they begin to crisp, approximately 1 minute. Place one hot fried oyster atop each canapé and drizzle with hollandaise. Serve at once.

MAKES 24 CANAPÉS

FRIED LOUISIANA OYSTERS WITH CREOLE MUSTARD HOLLANDAISE

Creole mustard, incorporating vinegar-marinated brown mustard seeds with a hint of horseradish, was made popular by Louisiana's German Creoles. The hot, zesty mustard (a mainstay in the Galatoire's kitchen) is readily available in the gourmet section of most American supermarkets. Its assertive nature cuts through the richness of the hollandaise sauce. A small dab of the Creole hollandaise is just the right foil for crisply fried oysters.

1 CUP HOLLANDAISE SAUCE (PAGE 249), AT ROOM TEMPERATURE

2 TABLESPOONS CREOLE MUSTARD OR ANY COARSE, GRAINY BROWN MUSTARD, AT ROOM TEMPERATURE

1 GALLON VEGETABLE OIL

4 CUPS YELLOW CORN FLOUR

1 TEASPOON SALT

1 TEASPOON FRESHLY GROUND BLACK PEPPER

4 DOZEN LARGE LOUISIANA OYSTERS

2 LEMONS, CUT INTO WEDGES, FOR GARNISH

2 TABLESPOONS CHOPPED FRESH CURLY PARSLEY, FOR GARNISH

In a small bowl, thoroughly blend the hollandaise with the Creole mustard. Set aside.

Heat the oil to 350°F in a large, heavy-bottomed pot suitable for frying.

Combine the corn flour, salt, and pepper in a mixing bowl. Dredge the oysters in the seasoned corn flour, shaking to remove excess flour. Fry the oysters for 3 to 4 minutes, or until they float to the surface and turn golden brown. Do not overcook. Remove with a slotted spoon and drain atop a platter lined with paper towels.

Serve the oysters at once, offering the Creole mustard hollandaise as a condiment with garnishes of lemon wedges and fresh parsley.

SERVES 10 TO 12

PAN-ROASTED DUCK BREAST WITH ORANGE DEMI-GLACE

This is a simple, modern adaptation of the classic French duck à l'orange that is relatively quick and easy to prepare.

1 CUP VEAL DEMI-GLACE (PAGE 267)

1 CUP FINE-QUALITY ORANGE MARMALADE

3 BONELESS DUCK BREASTS, APPROXIMATELY 6 OUNCES
    EACH

SALT AND FRESHLY GROUND BLACK PEPPER TO TASTE

ORANGE SLICES, FOR GARNISH

CHOPPED CURLY PARSLEY, FOR GARNISH

Heat the demi-glace and the marmalade in separate small sauté pans over medium heat until the demi-glace is liquid and the marmalade is melted, about 3 minutes. Strain the melted marmalade through a fine-mesh strainer. Discard the solids and add the liquid to the demi-glace. Reduce the sauce over medium-low heat for 4 to 5 minutes, until thick and syrupy. Set aside.

Season the duck breasts with salt and pepper. Sauté in a medium pan, skin side down, over medium heat for approximately 10 minutes, until the skin is golden brown and crispy. Turn the breasts and cook for an additional 4 to 5 minutes. Remove from the heat and allow the breasts to rest for 2 to 3 minutes before slicing, so that they will retain their juices.

Slice the duck on a diagonal into ¼-inch-thick slices. Fan the slices across a serving platter, skin side up. Nap the sauce across the duck breasts and garnish the platter with the orange slices and chopped parsley. Serve at once.

SERVES 6

SEARED RARE TUNA WITH CREOLE MUSTARD AND GREEN ONION EMULSION

This dish utilizes Galatoire's traditional French Creole culinary heritage as its underpinning while incorporating modern elements and preparation techniques. In true Galatoire's style, this dish is simple, elegant, and easy to prepare—perfect for entertaining. Prepare the emulsion in advance. Sear the tuna when ready to serve.

This dish would also be very appropriate as an appetizer or as a light summer entrée.

1 BUNCH OF SCALLIONS (GREEN PARTS ONLY), CHOPPED FINE (ABOUT ¾ CUP)

2 TABLESPOONS CHOPPED FRESH CURLY PARSLEY

½ CUP CREOLE MUSTARD OR ANY COARSE, GRAINY BROWN MUSTARD

¼ CUP HONEY

1 CUP RICE VINEGAR

2 LARGE EGG YOLKS

2 CUPS PLUS 2 TABLESPOONS EXTRA-VIRGIN OLIVE OIL

SALT AND FRESHLY GROUND BLACK PEPPER TO TASTE

2 POUNDS SUSHI-GRADE YELLOWFIN TUNA, LOIN OR STEAKS

3 LEMONS, CUT INTO WEDGES, FOR GARNISH (OPTIONAL)

Place all but ¼ cup of the scallions in a food processor with the parsley and purée. Stop the machine and add the mustard, honey, vinegar, and egg yolks. Resume processing. With the processor running, add 2 cups of the olive oil in a slow, steady stream to create the emulsion. Add salt and pepper to taste. Refrigerate while searing the tuna.

Preheat a cast-iron skillet over high heat. Cut the tuna into 2 × 2 × 6-inch strips and season with salt and pepper. Coat the bottom of the pan with the remaining 2 tablespoons of olive oil and heat through. Add the tuna and sear each of the four sides for approximately 45 seconds. If using tuna steaks instead of loin, sear the tuna on the top and bottom only. Remove the tuna from the pan and cool.

Slice the seared tuna into ¼-inch-thick pieces. The result will be 2 × 2 × ¼-inch pieces with a ring around the exterior where they have been seared and a beautiful rare interior. Arrange the tuna in a fan shape on a serving platter and drizzle with the Creole mustard and green onion emulsion. Take care to leave some of the rare tuna visible. Sprinkle the dish with the reserved finely chopped green onions and garnish with lemon wedges for color, if desired.

SERVES 10 TO 12

Hot Appetizers

GALATOIRE'S IS WELL KNOWN for its extensive and tantalizing first-course offerings, and many patrons concoct full meals from an assortment of these moderately sized, intensely flavorful dishes.

Bouchées d'Huitres ("little mouthfuls of oysters") were the Creole predecessor of many of Galatoire's popular appetizers such as Oysters Rockefeller, Oyster Confit, and Oysters en Brochette.

While the Seared Foie Gras with Savory Fruit Chutney you will find in this chapter is not seen on the restaurant's everyday menu, foie gras was once a staple on the Creole menu and, therefore, takes its rightful place here. The French brought the practice to New Orleans when they arrived here. A Creole woman is said to have amassed a fortune satisfying the tastes of local gourmands with the fatty livers of the geese she raised. Her farm was allegedly located near the site of today's Fairgrounds, which is now home to the annual New Orleans Jazz and Heritage Festival, another well-known venue for small, taster-size portions of fantastic New Orleans food.

ESCARGOTS BORDELAISE

Take care to thoroughly rinse the escargots under cold running water to remove all traces of the brine that could cloud their delicate flavor. The term "Bordelaise" in this dish refers to a classic New Orleans version consisting of butter or olive oil, garlic, and parsley. The simplicity lends itself to the escargots.

3 CUPS CLARIFIED BUTTER (PAGE 248)

1 CAN PREMIUM (72 COUNT) ESCARGOTS, RINSED AND
   PATTED DRY

6 TABLESPOONS FINELY CHOPPED FRESH GARLIC

¼ CUP CHOPPED CURLY PARSLEY

SALT AND FRESHLY GROUND BLACK PEPPER TO TASTE

Heat the clarified butter over medium heat in a large sauté pan. Add the escargots and cook for 2½ minutes, or until heated through. Add the garlic and sauté for another minute. Remove from the heat and stir in the parsley. Season with salt and pepper.

To serve, distribute the escargots and the Bordelaise sauce among 6 shallow bowls or gratin dishes and serve hot with warm New Orleans–style French bread.

SERVES 6

SAUTÉED SWEETBREAD MEDALLIONS WITH CHAMPAGNE AND CAPER BEURRE BLANC

In planning for this dish, take care to choose sweetbreads that are white, plump, and firm. They spoil quickly and should be prepared within twenty-four hours of purchase.

ONE 1½-POUND VEAL SWEETBREAD LOBE	1 POUND SALTED BUTTER, CUT INTO PIECES
1 TABLESPOON PLUS 1 TEASPOON BLACK PEPPERCORNS	3 TABLESPOONS NONPAREIL CAPERS, DRAINED
4 BAY LEAVES	1 TABLESPOON SALT
1 CUP CHAMPAGNE OR SPARKLING WINE	½ TABLESPOON FRESHLY GROUND WHITE PEPPER
JUICE FROM 1 LEMON (2 TABLESPOONS)	½ TABLESPOON FRESHLY GROUND BLACK PEPPER
1 TABLESPOON CHOPPED SHALLOTS	1 CUP ALL-PURPOSE FLOUR
1 TABLESPOON CHOPPED GARLIC	1 CUP CLARIFIED BUTTER (PAGE 248)

Place the sweetbread in a medium saucepan with 1 teaspoon of the peppercorns and the bay leaves. Add enough cold water to fully submerge the sweetbread. Bring to a boil over high heat, then lower heat to medium-high and cook for 5 minutes. The desired doneness is medium. The blanched sweetbread will be firm but will still give to the touch. Drain and set aside to cool.

To make the beurre blanc, set a small saucepan over medium heat. Add the champagne, lemon juice, the remaining 1 tablespoon peppercorns, the shallots, and garlic. Simmer for 5 minutes, or until reduced by one third. Whisking constantly, add the salted butter to the liquid one piece at a time until it has all been incorporated into the sauce. Remove from the heat and strain through a fine-mesh strainer into a fresh saucepan. Discard the solids. Add the capers to the strained sauce and set aside while you prepare the sweetbread.

When the sweetbread has cooled, use a small, sharp knife to remove the outer membrane. The sweetbread will be very fragile. Take extreme care as you cut it into twelve ¼-inch-thick medallions. Season them with the salt and black and white pepper and carefully dust with the flour. In a large sauté pan, heat the clarified butter over medium-high heat. The butter is hot enough when a small pinch of flour sizzles in the pan. Using a spatula, gently add the sweetbreads to the pan and sauté for 3½ minutes per side, until golden brown. Remove to a plate lined with paper towels to drain.

Divide the sautéed sweetbread medallions among 6 appetizer plates. Nap the beurre blanc across the center of the medallions, allowing some sauce to pool on the plate. The dish is most attractive when the capers are clustered at the centers of the medallions. Serve immediately.

SERVES 6

BRONZED GULF SHRIMP WITH ROASTED SQUASH AND PEPPERS,
TASSO, AND ROASTED GARLIC HOLLANDAISE

This dish thrilled some special clients and their guests when we created it for a private dinner party. The key to success here is to find the largest, most impressive shrimp available. Tasso is a very firm, extremely spicy, heavily smoked piece of lean pork that is commonly used as a seasoning meat in Cajun (not Creole) cooking. To make tasso, the pork, usually shoulder meat, is always slathered with cayenne pepper and sometimes other spices and seasonings, such as garlic and thyme. The meat, which is smoked for up to forty-eight hours, gives a powerful kick to red beans and rice, jambalaya, gumbo, and Cajun cream sauces.

For ease when entertaining, prepare the vegetables a day in advance and bring them to room temperature before assembling the dish.

1¼ CUPS OLIVE OIL	1 RED BELL PEPPER, CUT LENGTHWISE INTO QUARTERS
¼ CUP BALSAMIC VINEGAR	8 OUNCES TASSO, CUT INTO LARGE DICE
1 TABLESPOON SALT	2 TABLESPOONS FRESH THYME LEAVES
1 TABLESPOON FRESHLY GROUND BLACK PEPPER	10 GARLIC CLOVES
3 ZUCCHINI SQUASH, SCRUBBED AND CUT LENGTHWISE INTO QUARTERS	1 CUP HOLLANDAISE SAUCE (PAGE 249)
	2 DOZEN JUMBO (15 COUNT) SHRIMP WITH HEADS
3 YELLOW CROOKNECK SQUASH, SCRUBBED AND CUT LENGTHWISE INTO QUARTERS	¼ CUP CREOLE SEASONING (PAGE 257)
	4 TABLESPOONS (½ STICK) SALTED BUTTER

Preheat an outdoor grill or charcoal pit. In a large mixing bowl, combine ¼ cup of the olive oil, the balsamic vinegar, salt, and black pepper. Add the vegetables and toss to coat. Remove the vegetables, place on the grill, and cook each side for 3 minutes to obtain a caramel color. Remove the vegetables from the grill and chop into a large dice. Set aside.

Briefly heat a large sauté pan over high heat. Add the tasso, reduce the heat to medium-high, and cook for 3 minutes, or until the tasso begins to stick to the bottom of the pan. Add the chopped vegetables, including the liquid they have released, and the thyme. Simmer for 3 minutes. Set aside.

Place the garlic cloves in a small saucepan and cover with the remaining cup of olive oil. Cook over low heat for 10 minutes, or until the garlic is soft and has a faint caramel color. Remove the garlic from the oil and coarsely chop. Using the side of a large chef's knife, smash the garlic to make a paste.

Whisk 3 tablespoons of garlic paste into the hollandaise sauce. Mix until thoroughly incorporated. Set aside.

Carefully peel the inner rings of shell off of the shrimp, leaving the heads and tails attached. Season the partially peeled shrimp liberally with Creole seasoning. Melt the butter in a cast-iron skillet over high heat. Lay the shrimp in the skillet and cook for 3 minutes on each side, or until they appear to have been "bronzed."

Reheat the roasted vegetables and tasso and evenly divide among 6 plates, forming a mound at the center of each. Put four generous dollops of the garlic hollandaise between the mound of vegetables and the rim of each plate. Place a shrimp in each dollop of hollandaise and arrange so the heads are resting on the mound of roasted vegetables and tasso at the center of the plate. Serve at once.

SERVES 6

LOUISIANA CRAWFISH CAKE WITH CREOLE BEURRE BLANC

We thought this dish impressive enough to serve when we hosted a dinner at the venerable James Beard House in Manhattan, and we feature it on our everyday à la carte menu during crawfish season.

The succulent crawfish tails and aromatic seasonings bind together beautifully with minimal breading, and the beurre blanc adds a piquant gloss. The crawfish cakes can be formed a day in advance and refrigerated. Simply assemble the sauce and fry the crawfish cakes before serving. For an elegant brunch entrée, top the cakes with poached eggs and enjoy with a glass of champagne.

½ CUP CLARIFIED BUTTER (PAGE 248)	1 POUND SALTED BUTTER, CUT INTO PIECES (EACH PIECE
½ CUP MINCED RED BELL PEPPER	ABOUT 1 TABLESPOON)
½ CUP MINCED GREEN BELL PEPPER	¼ CUP MINCED ONION
¼ CUP MINCED YELLOW BELL PEPPER	¼ CUP MINCED CELERY
¼ CUP MINCED SCALLIONS (WHITE AND GREEN PARTS)	1 HEAPING TABLESPOON FRESH THYME LEAVES
1 POUND LOUISIANA CRAWFISH TAILS, PEELED	1 LEMON, QUARTERED (FOR JUICING)
1 TABLESPOON MINCED GARLIC	2 TABLESPOONS TOMATO PASTE
SALT AND CAYENNE PEPPER TO TASTE	1 TEASPOON TABASCO SAUCE
1 RECIPE BÉCHAMEL SAUCE (PAGE 251)	½ CUP WHITE WINE
3 LARGE EGG YOLKS	¼ CUP HEAVY CREAM
1 CUP SEASONED DRIED BREAD CRUMBS	

Heat ¼ cup of the clarified butter in a large sauté pan over medium-high heat. Add ¼ cup of the red bell pepper, ¼ cup of the green bell pepper, and all of the yellow bell pepper and scallions. Cook for 2 to 3 minutes, until the vegetables are tender. Add the crawfish tails and continue cooking for an additional 2 to 3 minutes, until heated through. Add the garlic and season with salt and cayenne. Fold in the béchamel sauce and cook for 4 to 5 minutes, until the mixture simmers. Use a rubber spatula to stir in the egg yolks and ½ cup of the bread crumbs. Remove the mixture from the heat and allow it to cool enough to touch, about 10 minutes. Divide the mixture into six equal portions and form into cakes. Roll the cakes evenly in the remaining ½ cup bread crumbs. Set aside.

In a medium saucepan over medium heat, melt 1 tablespoon of the salted butter. Add the remaining red and green bell peppers, the onions, and the celery and sauté for 5 to 7 minutes, until tender. Add the thyme and squeeze the lemon into the pan, discarding the lemon after juicing. Add the tomato paste and Tabasco and sauté for 1 minute longer.

Deglaze the pan with the white wine and cook for 8 to 10 minutes, until the mixture is reduced by half. Add the heavy cream and cook for an additional 6 to 8 minutes, until reduced by half again. Reduce the heat to low and add the remaining salted butter in small pieces, whisking constantly, until all has been incorporated. The sauce should be smooth and slightly thick. Strain the sauce, discard the solids, and set aside. Keep the sauce warm while you complete the crawfish cakes.

Heat the remaining ¼ cup clarified butter in a large sauté pan over low heat. Add the crawfish cakes and sauté for 2 minutes on each side, or until golden brown. Remove the cakes from the pan and drain on paper towels.

If the cakes were made in advance and refrigerated, the insides will still be cold so you will have to finish them in a 350°F oven for 6 to 8 minutes, until the centers are hot.

Ladle ¼ cup of the sauce in the center of an appetizer plate and center a crawfish cake atop the sauce. If a garnish is desired, some additional colored bell peppers can be cut into a ¼-inch dice and sprinkled around the plate like confetti.

SERVES 6

PETITE SOFT-SHELL CRABS WITH CRAWFISH BEURRE BLANC

"Soft-shell" is a term describing a growth state of the crab, during which time it casts off its shell to grow one that's larger. A couple of hours after the crab sheds its shell, its skin hardens into a new one. Fishermen must act quickly to harvest the crustaceans during the brief window of time when the shells are soft.

Choose only small crabs (also known as "buster" crabs) for this appetizer. They should be purchased alive as close to cooking time as possible. Set them on moist paper towels until ready to cook.

---

1 POUND LOUISIANA CRAWFISH TAILS, PEELED

1 CUP WHITE WINE

JUICE FROM 1 LEMON (2 TABLESPOONS)

1 TABLESPOON BLACK PEPPERCORNS

1 TABLESPOON CHOPPED SHALLOTS

1 TABLESPOON CHOPPED GARLIC

1 POUND SALTED BUTTER, CUT INTO ½-INCH PIECES

6 SMALL SOFT-SHELL CRABS

2 CUPS ALL-PURPOSE FLOUR

1 CUP CLARIFIED BUTTER (PAGE 248)

In a medium saucepan over medium heat, sauté half of the crawfish tails for 3 minutes, or until the tails and fat begin to brown in the pan. Add the white wine, lemon juice, peppercorns, shallots, and garlic and simmer for 5 minutes, or until reduced by one third. Whisking constantly, add the salted butter to the liquid one piece at a time until it has all been incorporated into the sauce. Remove the sauce from the heat and strain through a fine-mesh strainer into a fresh saucepan. Discard the solids, including the crawfish tails. Add the remaining crawfish to the strained sauce, then place the pan over low heat, stirring continuously, just until the crawfish are warmed through. Remove the pan from the heat and set aside while you prepare the crabs.

Clean the crabs by paring off the eyes and trimming the tails with a small, sharp knife. Gently pull back the shell on each side of the crab and then remove the gills underneath. Replace the shell.

Dredge the cleaned crabs in flour and shake off the excess. Add the clarified butter to a large sauté pan set over high heat. Sauté the crabs for 4 minutes per side, or until golden brown.

Center each crab on an appetizer plate and drizzle with the sauce, taking care to mound some crawfish tails gently atop each crab. Serve at once.

SERVES 6

FRIDAY REGULARS TAKING IT TO THE NEXT LEVEL: COUPLE WEDS
OVER LUNCH AT GALATOIRE'S

On Friday, May 7, 2004, New Orleanians Elizabeth Bowman and David Woolverton wed during a special luncheon celebration at Galatoire's. Eighty loved ones traveled from across the nation to join the couple on their special day.

"Lunch at Galatoire's," said Elizabeth Bowman just prior to her wedding, "that's what you're supposed to do in New Orleans, right? It's our favorite restaurant."

Elizabeth, a native of Greenwood, Missisippi, said Galatoire's was a favorite of her late mother, as well. "My parents lived in New Orleans when they were first married and, though they had little money, brunch at Galatoire's was their weekly treat after church on Sundays. Getting married at Galatoire's is a way for me to include my mother. She would have loved it."

Elizabeth said she and David had been in love for twenty-two years. "He's just the grandest thing I've ever laid eyes on," said the bride. The couple met when they were students at the University of Mississippi and had drifted in and out of one another's lives ever since.

Elizabeth recalled, "When David proposed to me he said, 'I have let you get away three times. Now I am going to kidnap you forever.' That's when I up and moved to New Orleans."

The couple chose a wedding menu that included Galatoire's classics: Shrimp Rémoulade, Crabmeat Maison, Oysters en Brochette, Turtle Soup au Sherry, Crabmeat Sardou, and Brabant Potatoes. Wedding cake and champagne were served for dessert.

"We are just so happy and excited," Elizabeth said on her wedding day, "we just want to shout about this from the mountaintop."

GRILLED QUAIL WITH CARAMELIZED VEGETABLES AND ANDOUILLE SAUSAGE

This modern dish, while a real deviation from what is typically offered at Galatoire's, remains true to our Creole heritage through the use of indigenous Louisiana ingredients. The inherent elegance of the grilled quail contrasts pleasantly with the assertive, smoky flavors the andouille lends to the vegetable medley. When planning for this dish, bear in mind that the quail must soak in the marinade overnight or up to twenty-four hours.

2 CUPS OLIVE OIL

½ CUP MINCED SCALLIONS (GREEN AND WHITE PARTS)

6 GARLIC CLOVES

2 BAY LEAVES

1 TABLESPOON FRESHLY GROUND BLACK PEPPER

6 SEMIBONELESS QUAIL (LEG AND WING BONES NOT REMOVED)

½ CUP (2½ OUNCES) FINELY DICED ANDOUILLE SAUSAGE

1 SMALL BUTTERNUT SQUASH, PEELED AND SEEDED, MEDIUM DICE

2 TABLESPOONS SALTED BUTTER

1 CUP MEDIUM-DICED YELLOW ONION

½ CUP MEDIUM-DICED RED BELL PEPPER

9 SPRIGS OF FRESH THYME, LEAVES REMOVED FROM 3 SPRIGS

1 TABLESPOON MINCED GARLIC

SALT AND CAYENNE PEPPER TO TASTE

1 CUP CHICKEN STOCK OR BROTH

VEGETABLE OIL, FOR GRILL

Combine the olive oil, scallions, garlic cloves, bay leaves, and black pepper in an airtight container. Submerge the quail in the marinade, cover, and refrigerate for at least 12 hours, but not more than 24.

In a large sauté pan, cook the andouille sausage over medium heat, stirring frequently, for 8 to 10 minutes, until it is crisp and the fat has been completely rendered. Remove the sausage from the pan with a slotted spoon, leaving the fat (there will be only a scant amount) in the pan. Add the butternut squash and sauté over medium heat. If the squash begins to stick, add up to 2 tablespoons of butter to the pan. Cook the squash down for 5 minutes, until just fork-tender. Add the onions and the bell peppers and cook for 8 to 10 minutes, until the onions begin to turn an even caramel color. Add the leaves of 3 sprigs of thyme and the garlic. Add the reserved andouille sausage and season with salt and cayenne. Sauté for 1 minute longer and deglaze the pan with the chicken stock or broth. Simmer for 5 minutes, or until most of the liquid has cooked out of the pan. Reduce the heat to low to keep the mixture warm while you grill the quail.

Heat an outdoor gas or charcoal grill until the coals are red hot and then brush the grill with a light coating of vegetable oil. Remove the quail from the marinade, pat dry with paper towels, and season with salt and pepper. Place the quail on the grill, breasts down. Cook for 2 minutes, or until the flesh is firm and opaque. Rotate one quarter turn and cook for another 2 minutes. This will create nice grill markings on the quail. Flip the quail and continue, taking care not to overcook. The quail is ready when it is firm to the touch, about 2 minutes more.

Mound the caramelized vegetables in the centers of 6 warm plates. Arrange the quail atop the vegetables. Garnish with the 6 remaining sprigs of fresh thyme. Serve at once.

SERVES 6

PANNED RABBIT TENDERLOIN AND SAUSAGE
OVER CARAMELIZED ONIONS

Yes, rabbit tenderloin, a delicacy that is common to both southern French and Louisiana Cajun cooking. This robust, flavorful dish can be made with commonly available green onion sausage if you are unable to find rabbit sausage. The decorative presentation offsets each of the individual components of the dish to its most appealing advantage.

1 LARGE ONION, JULIENNED	1½ POUNDS RABBIT SAUSAGE LINKS (ABOUT 6 LINKS)
3 TABLESPOONS OLIVE OIL	6 RABBIT TENDERLOINS
SALT AND FRESHLY GROUND BLACK PEPPER	2 CUPS ALL-PURPOSE FLOUR
FRESHLY GROUND WHITE PEPPER	2 CUPS SEASONED DRIED BREAD CRUMBS
2 CUPS HEAVY CREAM	2 LARGE EGGS
2 TABLESPOONS CREOLE MUSTARD OR ANY COARSE,	2 CUPS WHOLE MILK
GRAINY BROWN MUSTARD	2 CUPS CLARIFIED BUTTER (PAGE 248)

In a medium pan over high heat, sauté the onions in the olive oil. Cook the onions, stirring frequently, for 5 minutes, or until they become light brown in color. Deglaze the pan with ½ cup water and scrape with a wooden spoon to lift the caramelized onion bits from the pan. Reduce the heat to medium-high and allow it to simmer for 4 minutes, or until the liquid has evaporated. Sauté the onions for an additional 3 minutes and repeat the deglazing process with another ½ cup water. Simmer until the water has evaporated once again and the onions are very soft and a rich brown color. Season to taste with salt, black pepper, and white pepper. Set aside.

Add the cream to a medium saucepan and bring to a boil over high heat. Lower the heat to medium and simmer for 5 minutes, or until reduced by half. Stir in the mustard, 1 teaspoon salt, and ½ teaspoon black pepper. Reduce the heat to low to keep warm.

Preheat the broiler. Place the sausage pieces on a baking sheet. With the baking sheet on the second shelf of the oven, broil the sausage for 7 to 8 minutes, turning occasionally. The links should be cooked through, but not dry, and the outer skin will be brown and crispy. Set aside.

Cut each of the rabbit tenderloins into 2 pieces, then pound the pieces flat using a meat mallet. Combine 1 tablespoon salt, ½ tablespoon black pepper, and ½ tablespoon white pepper and use to season the tenderloins. Set up 3 mixing bowls. Add flour to one and bread crumbs to another. In the third bowl, whisk the eggs and milk to create an egg wash. Coat the tenderloins in flour and shake off the excess. Place them individually into the egg wash, ensuring that they are evenly coated. Remove the tenderloins from the egg wash. Allow the excess wash to drain off and coat the tenderloins evenly with the bread crumbs.

Add the clarified butter to a large sauté pan over medium-high heat. Add the rabbit tenderloins and sauté for 4 minutes per side, or until golden brown. Remove from the pan to a platter lined with paper towels. Pat the tenderloins with the paper towels to remove the excess oil.

Evenly divide the caramelized onions among 6 plates, creating a mound in the center of each plate. Cut each sausage into 2 pieces on an extreme diagonal, nearly end to end. Place the end of the sausage at the bottom of the mound of onions, pointed ends up. Nap the mustard sauce on the plate at the base of the onion mound. Slice the panned rabbit tenderloin and fan the slices over the sauce. Serve immediately.

SERVES 6

SEARED FOIE GRAS WITH SAVORY FRUIT CHUTNEY

The sweet and savory flavor of the chutney (which can be prepared up to one day in advance) cuts beautifully through the warm, rich intensity of the foie gras. The flavors and textures of this dish are very dissimilar, though highly complimentary. This memorable appetizer is made ever more so when it is served with a golden Sauternes or other sweet white wine. Though it is now savored internationally, foie gras ("fat liver") was originally a specialty of the Alsace and Perigord regions of France.

1 TABLESPOON SALTED BUTTER

½ CUP FINELY CHOPPED SCALLIONS (WHITE AND GREEN PARTS)

½ CUP DICED BOSC PEAR

½ CUP DICED MANGO

½ CUP PITTED, CHOPPED BLACK CHERRIES

1 TABLESPOON CHOPPED GARLIC

1 TABLESPOON FRESH THYME LEAVES

½ CUP CHAMPAGNE VINEGAR

SALT AND FRESHLY GROUND BLACK PEPPER TO TASTE

ONE 1-POUND LOBE OF FOIE GRAS

6 SPRIGS OF FRESH THYME

Melt the butter in a medium sauté pan over high heat. Sauté the scallions for 3 minutes, or until translucent. Add the pears, mangoes, and cherries and sauté for an additional 3 minutes. Reduce the heat to medium-high and add the garlic and thyme leaves and sauté for 1 minute. Add the vinegar and simmer for 2 to 3 minutes, until the liquid has evaporated. Season with salt and pepper. Chill if preparing in advance or set aside to come to room temperature.

Slice the foie gras lobe into 6 large slices, ½ inch to ¾ inch thick. Etch a decorative diamond pattern onto one side of each slice using the point of a paring knife to score shallow parallel lines (½ inch apart) across the slices. Turn the slices a quarter turn and score with another set of parallel lines to form the pattern. Set a large nonstick skillet over high heat. The pan is ready when a drop of water sizzles and vaporizes on contact. Place the scored side of the foie gras down and sear for 45 seconds. Gently turn to the other side and sear for an additional 45 seconds. Do not overcrowd the pan. Cook in 2 batches if necessary, discarding rendered fat between batches. Remove from the pan and plate immediately.

Evenly divide the chutney among 6 warm appetizer plates. Form a mound at the center of each plate and gently lay the foie gras atop, scored side up. Insert a sprig of fresh thyme into the foie gras as a garnish. Serve at once.

SERVES 6

Oyster Pan Roast

The oysters plump as they absorb the flavors of the rich, creamy sauce. Though impressive, the dish is quick and easy to prepare, making it an ideal choice for entertaining, particularly during the Thanksgiving and Christmas holidays when southern oysters are at their peak.

1 TABLESPOON SALTED BUTTER

1 CUP DICED ONION

1/2 CUP DICED SHALLOTS

1/4 CUP FINELY CHOPPED SCALLIONS (WHITE AND GREEN PARTS)

36 LARGE GULF OYSTERS, SHUCKED

3 TABLESPOONS CHOPPED GARLIC

1/2 CUP WHITE WINE

1 CUP HEAVY CREAM

1/2 CUP GRATED PARMESAN CHEESE

SALT AND FRESHLY GROUND WHITE PEPPER TO TASTE

1 CUP SEASONED DRIED BREAD CRUMBS

1/2 CUP CLARIFIED BUTTER (PAGE 248)

Melt the salted butter in a medium sauté pan over high heat. Sauté the onions, shallots, and scallions for 3 minutes, or until translucent. Add the oysters and sauté over high heat for 1 minute, or until the edges start to curl slightly. Reduce the heat to medium-high and add the garlic and sauté for 1 minute more. Add the white wine, swirl the pan to deglaze, and allow the mixture to simmer for 2 minutes. Add the heavy cream and simmer all ingredients for 4 to 6 minutes, until the cream is bubbling and the sauce begins to reduce. Remove the pan from the heat and stir in the Parmesan cheese. Season with salt and white pepper.

Preheat the broiler. Evenly divide the oysters and sauce among 6 individual casserole dishes. The oysters should not be fully submerged beneath the sauce. Sprinkle with bread crumbs, drizzle with clarified butter, and broil for 1 to 2 minutes, until golden. Serve at once.

SERVES 6

OYSTERS ROCKEFELLER

Over the years many of the city's institutions have developed their own variations on the rich, herbaceous dish that was originally created in New Orleans in 1899 by chef and restaurateur Jules Alciatore of Antoine's Restaurant and named for the wealthy and unforgettable John D. Rockefeller. Like Rockefeller's philanthropic legacy, the timeless dish named for him lives on through the ages.

If you must cook the oysters in batches, the rock salt will help to retain the heat within the first batches while the other batches cook.

If Herbsaint is unavailable in your area you may substitute Pernod.

¾ CUP CHOPPED FENNEL (BULB ONLY)

¼ CUP CHOPPED LEEKS (GREEN AND WHITE PARTS)

¼ CUP FINELY CHOPPED CURLY PARSLEY

¼ CUP FINELY CHOPPED SCALLIONS (GREEN AND WHITE PARTS)

¼ CUP CHOPPED CELERY

¼ CUP KETCHUP

1½ CUPS COOKED AND DRAINED CHOPPED FROZEN SPINACH

½ TEASPOON SALT

½ TEASPOON FRESHLY GROUND WHITE PEPPER

½ TEASPOON CAYENNE PEPPER

1 TEASPOON DRIED THYME LEAVES

1 TEASPOON GROUND ANISE

2 TEASPOONS WORCESTERSHIRE SAUCE

¼ CUP HERBSAINT LIQUEUR

1 CUP (2 STICKS) MELTED SALTED BUTTER

½ CUP SEASONED DRIED BREAD CRUMBS

12 CUPS ROCK SALT

6 DOZEN OYSTERS ON THE HALF SHELL

12 LEMON WEDGES

Preheat the oven to 350°F.

To make the sauce, in a food processor combine the fennel, leeks, parsley, scallions, celery, ketchup, spinach, salt, white pepper, cayenne, thyme, anise, Worcestershire, and Herbsaint. Purée the mixture thoroughly. Using a rubber spatula, scrape the contents of the food processor into a large mixing bowl. Stir in the butter and the bread crumbs. Ensure that the mixture is well blended.

Pour enough rock salt into twelve 8-inch cake pans to cover the bottoms of the pans. Arrange 6 oysters in their half shells in each pan.

Fill a pastry bag with the Rockefeller sauce and pipe equal portions of the sauce over each shell. If you do not have a pastry bag, use a large tablespoon to distribute the sauce. Place the pans in the oven and bake for 5 minutes, or until the sauce sets. Turn the heat up to broil and broil the oysters for an additional 3 to 4 minutes, until the tops are bubbling.

It may be necessary to bake the oysters in batches.

Line each of 12 dinner plates with cloth napkins that have been folded into neat squares. Carefully nestle the pans of oysters within the folded napkins. Garnish with lemon wedges and serve at once.

SERVES 12

OYSTER CONFIT

This simple, quick dish is just the thing to get family dinner gatherings off to a flavorful start. Pull out the oven mitts, pull the pan right from the oven, and pass the dish, family-style, around the table. The oysters poach in the fragrant oil and the herbs and juices shout to be mopped up with plenty of French bread—either New Orleans style or the traditional French baguette.

3 CUPS EXTRA-VIRGIN OLIVE OIL	36 LARGE GULF OYSTERS, SHUCKED, WITH LIQUID
3 TABLESPOONS CHOPPED GARLIC	(OYSTER LIQUOR)
3 TABLESPOONS FRESH THYME LEAVES	2 TABLESPOONS CRACKED BLACK PEPPER
3 TABLESPOONS CHOPPED FRESH OREGANO	3 TABLESPOONS FRESHLY GRATED PARMESAN CHEESE

Preheat the oven to 300°F. Gently mix the olive oil, garlic, thyme, oregano, oysters, and oyster liquor in a roasting pan. Sprinkle the cracked pepper and the Parmesan cheese over the mixture. Bake for 12 to 15 minutes, until the edges of the oysters begin to curl and the oysters begin to plump up. Serve immediately while piping hot.

SERVES 6

OYSTERS EN BROCHETTE

The juices from the bacon seep into the oysters in the frying process, which gives them a sweet, smoky flavor. The final result is a heavenly morsel that is crisp and crunchy on the outside, and bursting with smoky, briny flavors inside. It has been a favorite at Galatoire's from the very beginning. You will need six wooden skewers for this recipe. Trim them if they are too long to fit in your frying pan.

---

1 GALLON VEGETABLE OIL

12 THICK SLICES SMOKED BACON, CUT IN HALF (24 HALF PIECES)

36 LARGE OYSTERS, SHUCKED

2 LARGE EGGS

2 CUPS WHOLE MILK

2 CUPS ALL-PURPOSE FLOUR

1 RECIPE MEUNIÈRE BUTTER (PAGE 263)

6 TOAST POINTS, FOR GARNISH

6 LEMON WEDGES, FOR GARNISH

Heat the oil to 350°F in a large sauté pan, taking care to maintain the temperature. In a separate, medium sauté pan, cook the bacon over medium heat for 3 to 4 minutes to render some of the fat from the meat. The bacon should be lightly browned but still pliable. Drain on paper towels. To assemble the brochettes, skewer 1 piece of bacon, then 2 oysters. Repeat twice and add 1 more slice of bacon for a total of 4 pieces of bacon and 6 oysters on each skewer. Repeat the process for all 6 skewers. Set aside.

In a medium bowl, whisk together the eggs and milk to make an egg wash. Place the flour in a shallow baking pan. Dip the skewers into the wash. Allow the excess liquid to drip off. Put the brochettes into the pan of flour and coat heavily. Shake off the excess flour and place the brochettes into the hot oil. Fry the brochettes for 4 to 5 minutes, until they are golden and float to the top. Do not overcook the oysters. Remove from the oil to a plate lined with paper towels.

Place the brochettes at the centers of 6 appetizer plates. Hold one end of the brochette to the plate. Grasp the other end with a paper towel and slide the skewer out of the brochette. Nap the meunière butter over the top of the oysters, allowing the sauce to pool at the bottom of the plate. Garnish each dish with a toast point and a wedge of lemon.

SERVES 6

Southern Salads and Cold Appetizers

The time from late May through early October is notoriously hot and humid in New Orleans, with temperatures into the nineties almost daily. The humidity, which often hovers near 100 percent, can feel as oppressive as a dictator, and up to eleven hours of sunshine a day leaves everyone preoccupied with trying to stay cool. The heat affects every aspect of life in New Orleans. Woolen clothing is rejected in favor of featherweight cottons and linens. Woven rugs are rolled away and replaced by sisal mats, or floors are left bare. Upholstered furnishings are draped in protective cotton slipcovers.

Beginning with the season's first real heat wave, the foods people eat are a direct reflection of the temperature outside. Complex, heavy soups, gumbos, stews, and cuts of meat are rejected in favor of light, sprightly dishes with clear, straightforward flavors.

Area bayous, marshlands, and waterways pour forth a warm-weather abundance of fresh shrimp, crab, oysters, and fish, which lend themselves well to a light touch and a cool chill.

A century of honoring patron requests for special cold salads—tossed as well as composed—has endowed Galatoire's with an extensive repertoire of cool selections, which can be enjoyed either in addition to or in place of traditional hot meals.

We appreciate and enjoy the intensity of color, delicate flavors, and novelty of popular "designer" lettuce varieties, and we put them to good use at Galatoire's. However, we would like to plead a case for the lowly, humble iceberg lettuce called for in several of the recipes you will see in this section.

While some might regard it as boring, this old workhorse is the only one of its class with the crisp texture and clean flavor needed to offset the assertive tang you will find in many of our signature dressings.

Also, you will find that Creole mustard is a common ingredient in many of our cold presentations. It is distinguished not only by its coarse, grainy texture but also by the light tang it derives from the addition of prepared horseradish. We use Zatarain's brand Creole mustard at Galatoire's. It is readily available in most American supermarkets.

When working with jumbo lump crabmeat, take extreme care not to break up the lumps.

AVOCADO STUFFED WITH CRABMEAT

For variation, substitute creamy Crabmeat Maison (page 86) for jumbo lump crabmeat.

3 SOFT, RIPE AVOCADOS, PREFERABLY HASS

1 HEAD OF ICEBERG LETTUCE, WASHED, DRIED, AND CUT
   INTO LARGE RIBBONS

1 POUND JUMBO LUMP CRABMEAT

1 LARGE VINE-RIPENED TOMATO, CUT INTO 6 WEDGES

1 CUP CREOLE MUSTARD VINAIGRETTE (PAGE 258)

Slice the avocados in half lengthwise and remove the pits. Peel and set the 6 halves aside.

Create a bed of lettuce on 6 chilled plates. Nest the avocado halves in the centers of the lettuce-covered plates. Evenly divide the crabmeat into the cavities of the avocados, forming mounds. Add a wedge of tomato to each plate and drizzle the vinaigrette atop the crabmeat, avocado, tomato, and lettuce. Serve at once.

SERVES 6

Bibb Lettuce with Creamy Roasted Garlic Vinaigrette and Goat Cheese Croutons

This fresh, sprightly dish takes a modern approach to the salade composée, *while remaining true to its distinctly French heritage.*

---

3 SHALLOTS

ICE WATER

12 ¼-INCH BREAD ROUNDS (FROM ABOUT ½ 12-INCH
    FRENCH BAGUETTE)

4 OUNCES CHÈVRE (GOAT) CHEESE, SOFTENED

3 HEADS OF BIBB LETTUCE, CUT INTO QUARTERS,
    RINSED, AND DRIED

1 RECIPE CREAMY ROASTED GARLIC VINAIGRETTE
    (PAGE 255)

Preheat the oven to 350°F.

While the oven is heating, slice the shallots into thin rings and soak the rings in ice water while you make the croutons. This will soften their flavor and make them appealingly crunchy.

Place the French-bread rounds on a cookie sheet and bake for 3 to 4 minutes, until they are a pale golden color. Remove the croutons from the oven and spread them with the softened goat cheese. Return the croutons to the oven to warm the cheese for 3 to 4 minutes, until the top is lightly browned.

Divide the lettuce wedges equally among 6 chilled salad plates and ladle the dressing over the lettuce. Remove the shallot rings from the ice bath, pat dry with a paper towel, and divide the rings atop the lettuce quarters. Garnish each salad with 2 cheese croutons.

SERVES 6

BLUE CHEESE AND PECAN STUFFED QUAIL SALAD

This absolutely gorgeous salade composée *was created at the request of a special patron for a privately hosted dinner. In that setting we featured it as one of five courses. Such a presentation would be appropriate for a robust holiday dinner. However, the salad also works as an appetizer and it is hearty enough to stand alone as a light meal, in which case we recommend that you increase the servings to two quail per person.*

1 CUP BALSAMIC VINEGAR

1 SPRIG OF FRESH ROSEMARY

1 GARLIC CLOVE, PEELED AND HALVED

2 TABLESPOONS HONEY

1 TABLESPOON CORNSTARCH

6 SEMIBONELESS QUAIL (LEG AND WING BONES NOT REMOVED)

2 TABLESPOONS WORCESTERSHIRE SAUCE

SALT AND FRESHLY GROUND BLACK PEPPER TO TASTE

2 TABLESPOONS SALTED BUTTER

½ POUND BLUE CHEESE, SOFTENED AND CRUMBLED

¼ CUP CHOPPED SPICY PECANS (PAGE 264), PLUS ADDITIONAL SPICY PECAN HALVES FOR GARNISH

2 LARGE VINE-RIPENED TOMATOES, SLICED ½ INCH THICK

2 BELGIAN ENDIVES, CUT LENGTHWISE INTO SIXTHS (12 PIECES TOTAL)

¼ CUP EXTRA-VIRGIN OLIVE OIL

In a small sauté pan over medium heat, cook the balsamic vinegar with the rosemary and garlic for 5 minutes, or until it is reduced by half. Remove the rosemary and garlic and whisk in the honey. Dissolve the cornstarch in 2 tablespoons of water and slowly whisk it into the pan, 1 tablespoon at a time, until a syrupy consistency that coats the back of a spoon is achieved. Remove the syrup from the heat and set aside.

Preheat the oven to 350°F.

In a medium mixing bowl, toss the quail in the Worcestershire sauce. Allow it to sit for 5 minutes. Season the quail with salt and pepper.

Melt the butter in a large nonstick pan over high heat. Place the quail, breasts down, in the hot pan. Reduce the heat to medium and cook for 2 to 3 minutes, until the breasts begin to brown. The Worcestershire will give the skins a dark lacquered look, so you must continuously move and check the quail to ensure that the skins don't burn. Flip the quail and cook for an additional 1 to 2 minutes, until the flesh is firm and opaque. If the cooking pan is not oven-safe, transfer the quail into an oven-safe container. Place the quail in the oven and bake for an additional 6 minutes, or until the skins are brown and crisp. Remove the quail from the oven to a wire rack to cool.

Mix the blue cheese and chopped spicy pecans together in a bowl. Divide the mixture into 6 portions and mold them into balls. Each should be about the size of a golf ball. Stuff the blue cheese and pecan mixture into the breast cavities of the partially cooled quail.

Return the stuffed quail to the 350°F oven for 3 to 4 minutes to reheat the quail and warm the cheese. When the cheese begins to ooze from the quail, remove them from the oven.

Divide the sliced tomatoes among 6 chilled plates and season with salt and pepper. Arrange 2 pieces of Belgian endive on the plates, next to the tomatoes. Drizzle the tomatoes and endive with olive oil. Use a spatula to scoop up the quail and any blue cheese that may have melted out. Place the stuffed quail and cheese directly atop the sliced tomatoes. Garnish the plate with the balsamic syrup and pecan halves. Serve at once.

SERVES 6

CRABMEAT MAISON

Galatoire's utilizes up to 750 pounds of jumbo lump crabmeat each week—much of which is used in the preparation of this favorite dish. In its composition, briny fresh lumps of sweet, succulent blue crab are gently folded with a simple sauce that is at once luscious and bracing. Only the finest-quality jumbo lump crab should be used for this elegant dish, which is perfect as a salad or cold appetizer but also makes for a lovely luncheon entrée.

2 LARGE EGG YOLKS

2 TABLESPOONS RED WINE VINEGAR

1 TABLESPOON CREOLE MUSTARD OR ANY COARSE,
   GRAINY BROWN MUSTARD

1 TEASPOON FRESH LEMON JUICE

1 CUP VEGETABLE OIL

¼ CUP NONPAREIL CAPERS, DRAINED

¼ CUP CHOPPED SCALLIONS (GREEN AND WHITE PARTS)

1 TABLESPOON CHOPPED CURLY PARSLEY

SALT AND FRESHLY GROUND WHITE PEPPER TO TASTE

1 POUND JUMBO LUMP CRABMEAT

1 SMALL HEAD OF ICEBERG LETTUCE, WASHED, DRIED,
   AND CUT INTO THIN RIBBONS

2 MEDIUM VINE-RIPENED TOMATOES, CORED AND CUT
   INTO SIX 1-INCH-THICK SLICES

Combine the egg yolks, vinegar, mustard, and lemon juice in a food processor and process for 2 minutes. With the processor running, add the oil slowly in a thin stream and process until emulsified. Remove to a mixing bowl and gently fold in the capers, scallions, and parsley. Season with salt and white pepper. Chill for 2 to 4 hours. Just before serving, gently fold in the crabmeat, taking care not to break up the lumps.

Divide the lettuce among 6 serving plates and top with a slice of tomato. Spoon the crab atop the tomato and serve.

SERVES 6

Vine-Ripened Tomatoes Stuffed with Boiled Shrimp

This salad is light and flavorful and makes a delicious starter for a summer dinner or stands alone as a luncheon entrée.

6 MEDIUM VINE-RIPENED TOMATOES

SALT AND FRESHLY GROUND BLACK PEPPER TO TASTE

1 HEAD OF ICEBERG LETTUCE, WASHED, DRIED, AND CUT
   INTO LARGE RIBBONS

3 DOZEN JUMBO (15 COUNT) BOILED SHRIMP, PEELED

1 CUP HOMEMADE MAYONNAISE (PAGE 259)

1 CUP CREOLE MUSTARD VINAIGRETTE (PAGE 258)

3 LEMONS, CUT INTO WEDGES, FOR GARNISH

Using a paring knife, make a circular cut around the top of each tomato. Discard the core of each tomato and remove enough of the interior to create a cup that is about ½ inch deep. Season the inside of each tomato cup with salt and black pepper. Set aside.

Create a bed of lettuce on 6 chilled plates and nest the tomato cups in the centers of the lettuce beds. Hook 6 shrimp on the sides of each tomato cup. Put a dollop of homemade mayonnaise in the center of each tomato cup and drizzle the entirety with the vinaigrette dressing. Garnish with lemon wedges and grind a bit of fresh black pepper atop the mayonnaise.

SERVES 6

DINKELSPIEL SALAD

This colorful salade composée *was created in the 1920s for longtime patron Manuel Dinkelspiel. It was retired from the menu in the 1960s but was recently reintroduced as part of the restaurant's 100th anniversary celebration.*

---

6 LARGE EGGS

SALT TO TASTE

36 ANCHOVY FILLETS

2 HEADS ICEBERG LETTUCE, WASHED, DRIED, AND CUT INTO ¼-INCH RIBBONS

1 POUND JUMBO LUMP CRABMEAT

3 DOZEN LARGE (21–25 COUNT) SHRIMP, BOILED AND PEELED

2 LARGE VINE-RIPENED TOMATOES, CUT INTO 1-INCH SQUARES

1 CUP CREOLE MUSTARD VINAIGRETTE (PAGE 258)

FRESHLY GROUND BLACK PEPPER TO TASTE

In a small pot, place the eggs with a pinch of salt and bring to a boil. Boil the eggs for 8 minutes. Take care not to overcook the eggs or you will lose the beautiful yellow color of the yolk. Remove them from the heat. Run cool water into the pot to cool the eggs. Carefully peel the boiled eggs, then cut them in half lengthwise, and remove the yolks. Set the yolks aside.

Place 2 anchovies atop one another. Starting at one end, roll the anchovies into a coil. Place the curled anchovies into the "cup" of the egg white half, where the yolk was. Repeat with the remaining anchovies and egg whites. Set aside.

Divide the shredded lettuce into the centers of 6 chilled salad plates. Equally divide the crabmeat among the plates, creating mounds in the centers of the lettuce beds. Place 6 boiled shrimp around the crabmeat on each plate. Place pieces of tomato between each shrimp. Place 2 anchovy-stuffed egg halves on the sides of each plate. Place an egg yolk atop the crabmeat and then crisscross 2 anchovies atop the yolk. Drizzle the creole mustard vinaigrette over the salads, and season with salt and pepper. Serve at once.

SERVES 6

GALATOIRE'S SALADE MAISON

For a variation on this popular salad, creamy Blue Cheese Dressing (page 253) may be substituted and white asparagus may be used in place of the green variety.

---

12 FRESH GREEN ASPARAGUS SPEARS

ICE WATER

6 CUPS MESCLUN LETTUCE MIX, RINSED, DRAINED, AND
   DRIED

1 LARGE VINE-RIPENED TOMATO, CUT INTO 1-INCH DICE

1 CUP CREOLE MUSTARD VINAIGRETTE (PAGE 258)

6 ANCHOVY FILLETS

3 HARD-BOILED EGGS, CHOPPED

Steam the asparagus spears in a double boiler for 5 to 6 minutes, until tender but not mushy. Remove the spears from the steamer and chill in an ice-water bath for 5 minutes. Remove the spears from the ice bath, dry, and set aside.

Place the mesclun mix in a large mixing bowl with the tomatoes. Add the vinaigrette and toss until all of the leaves are evenly coated.

Evenly divide the salad among 6 chilled salad plates. Place 2 asparagus spears in the shape of an "X" atop each salad. Lay an anchovy fillet over the asparagus. Sprinkle the eggs over the top of the salads and serve.

SERVES 6

GREEN SALAD WITH GARLIC

Not a popular choice with young romantics, but embraced heartily by all others . . .

2 TABLESPOONS FRESHLY MINCED GARLIC

¼ CUP EXTRA-VIRGIN OLIVE OIL

6 CUPS MESCLUN LETTUCE MIX, RINSED, DRAINED, AND DRIED

1 CUP CREOLE MUSTARD VINAIGRETTE (PAGE 258)

Place the garlic in a small serving container and add the olive oil. Place the mesclun in a large mixing bowl, add the creole vinaigrette, and toss until all of the leaves are evenly coated.

Evenly divide the salad among 6 chilled salad plates. Drizzle with the garlic and olive oil mixture and serve.

SERVES 6

GODCHAUX SALAD

Back in the 1920s, each day Mr. Leon Godchaux would make the short walk to Galatoire's from his family's elegant namesake department store on Canal Street. Overheated from the walk, in the warmer months Mr. Godchaux would request that a salad containing all of his favorite things be composed just for him. Over the years Mr. Godchaux's eponymous salad has become a mainstay on the Galatoire's menu.

The bright, acidic tang of the Creole mustard–based dressing cuts cleanly through the richness of the lump crabmeat, shrimp, and hard-boiled eggs. Only iceberg lettuce should be used for the Godchaux salad; its crisp texture is necessary to balance the dish.

1 MEDIUM HEAD OF ICEBERG LETTUCE, WASHED, DRIED, AND TORN INTO BITE-SIZE PIECES

2 VINE-RIPENED TOMATOES, CORED AND CUT INTO LARGE BITE-SIZE PIECES

1 POUND JUMBO LUMP CRABMEAT, CLEANED

30 LARGE (21–25 COUNT) SHRIMP, BOILED AND PEELED

CREOLE MUSTARD VINAIGRETTE (PAGE 258)

3 HARD-BOILED EGGS, CHOPPED

12 ANCHOVY FILLETS

In a large bowl, combine the lettuce, tomatoes, crabmeat, and shrimp. Gradually add the dressing to the salad, according to your preference, and toss gently until all ingredients are well coated.

Divide the salad mixture onto 6 chilled plates. Garnish each salad with chopped egg and 2 anchovy fillets. Extra dressing can be served on the side.

SERVES 6

HEART OF LETTUCE WITH
JUMBO LUMP CRABMEAT VINAIGRETTE

Iceberg lettuce features heavy, round, tightly packed heads of pale green leaves. It is crisp, succulent, and wilt-resistant and stands up admirably to dressings. The neutral, though pleasant, flavor of iceberg lettuce allows the herbs and the delicate briny flavor of the prized crabmeat to shine through.

¾ CUP EXTRA-VIRGIN OLIVE OIL	SALT AND FRESHLY GROUND BLACK PEPPER TO TASTE
¼ CUP CHAMPAGNE VINEGAR	¼ CUP GRATED PARMESAN CHEESE
2 TEASPOONS FRESH LEMON JUICE	1 POUND JUMBO LUMP CRABMEAT
½ TEASPOON FRESH THYME LEAVES	2 HEADS OF ICEBERG LETTUCE
½ TEASPOON CHOPPED FRESH OREGANO	3 LEMONS, CUT INTO WEDGES, FOR GARNISH
1 TEASPOON FRESHLY MINCED GARLIC	

Place the olive oil, vinegar, lemon juice, thyme, oregano, garlic, salt, and pepper in a mixing bowl and whisk vigorously. Add the Parmesan cheese and whisk again. Gently fold the crabmeat into the vinaigrette, taking care not to break the lumps. Chill.

While the crab dressing is chilling, slice the tops and bottoms off of the lettuce heads, then cut three 1-inch-thick slices of lettuce hearts from each head of lettuce. Wash, dry, and set aside. Reserve the remaining lettuce for another use.

Center the hearts of lettuce on 6 chilled salad plates. Using a large slotted spoon, gently stir the crabmeat vinaigrette and equally divide the crabmeat atop the centers of the lettuce hearts. Drizzle a desired amount of the remaining dressing on the rest of the hearts. Garnish with lemon wedges and serve.

SERVES 6

Marinated Avocado, Crawfish, and Crab Salad

This salad would make an impressive starter to an outdoor summer dinner. The marinated seafood and avocado salad can be completed one hour before guests arrive. All that is left to do is spoon the mixture atop the lettuce and garnish the salad when you are ready to serve.

---

2 SOFT RIPE AVOCADOS, PREFERABLY HASS

1 CUP CREOLE MUSTARD VINAIGRETTE (PAGE 258)

½ POUND JUMBO LUMP CRABMEAT

½ POUND FRESH, PEELED LOUISIANA CRAWFISH TAILS

2 TABLESPOONS CHOPPED FRESH CURLY PARSLEY

4 HEADS BUTTER LETTUCE, TORN INTO BITE-SIZE PIECES, WASHED AND DRIED

½ CUP EXTRA-VIRGIN OLIVE OIL

SALT AND FRESHLY GROUND BLACK PEPPER TO TASTE

6 HEARTS OF PALM, RINSED AND DRIED

Slice the avocados in half lengthwise, remove the pit, and peel them. Chop the avocados into a large dice, about ½ inch. Place them in a small bowl and add the vinaigrette. Toss, and refrigerate for 2 hours.

Add the crabmeat, crawfish, and parsley to the avocado. Fold the mixture, taking care not to break the lumps of crabmeat or to mash the soft avocado. Chill the mixture for 2 hours.

In a large mixing bowl combine the lettuce, the olive oil, and salt and pepper. Toss the mixture until the leaves are evenly coated. Slice the hearts of palm on a bias, end to end, making long triangular shapes.

Create a bed of lettuce on 6 chilled plates. Evenly distribute the avocado, crawfish, and crab salad atop the lettuce. Lean 2 slices of hearts of palm against the avocado salad. Serve.

SERVES 6

SHRIMP RÉMOULADE

Shrimp rémoulade is in every New Orleans girl's arsenal of favored dishes for relaxed entertaining. Serve this simple dish on elegant china and it's fit for a king—Mardi Gras or otherwise. This is our most popular dish and most frequently requested recipe. Bonus for the home cook: The sauce is definitely best made a day in advance and refrigerated, then all that's left to do is toss in the shrimp, and plate and serve. It's a snap to make, yet it's always impressive.

³⁄₄ CUP CHOPPED CELERY

³⁄₄ CUP CHOPPED SCALLIONS (WHITE AND GREEN PARTS)

¹⁄₂ CUP CHOPPED CURLY PARSLEY

1 CUP CHOPPED YELLOW ONION

¹⁄₂ CUP KETCHUP

¹⁄₂ CUP TOMATO PURÉE

¹⁄₂ CUP CREOLE MUSTARD OR ANY COARSE, GRAINY
   BROWN MUSTARD

2 TABLESPOONS PREPARED HORSERADISH, OR TO TASTE

¹⁄₄ CUP RED WINE VINEGAR

2 TABLESPOONS SPANISH HOT PAPRIKA

1 TEASPOON WORCESTERSHIRE SAUCE

¹⁄₂ CUP SALAD OIL

4 DOZEN JUMBO (15 COUNT) SHRIMP, PEELED, BOILED,
   AND CHILLED

1 SMALL HEAD OF ICEBERG LETTUCE, WASHED, DRIED,
   AND CUT INTO THIN RIBBONS

Mince the celery, scallions, parsley, and onions in a food processor. Add the ketchup, tomato purée, Creole mustard, horseradish, red wine vinegar, paprika, and Worcestershire. Begin processing again and add the oil in a slow drizzle to emulsify. Stop when the dressing is smooth. Chill for 6 to 8 hours or overnight. Correct the seasoning with additional horseradish, if desired, after the ingredients have had the opportunity to marry.

In a large mixing bowl, add the sauce to the shrimp and toss gently to coat. Divide the lettuce among 6 chilled salad plates. Divide the shrimp evenly atop the lettuce and serve.

SERVES 6

THE CLAVERIES

When my husband, Philip, went off to college in 1959, his mother, Viola, became very lonely and sad. Her only child was now living a thousand miles away in Princeton, New Jersey, and while she was very proud of him, she missed her weekends filled with Country Day School football games and basketball games and other teen and family events. In an effort to cheer up the "empty nester," my father-in-law, Louis Claverie, invited Viola to have lunch at Galatoire's. They had so much fun that they continued their Saturday lunch date at Galatoire's . . . until 1977, when our son, Philip, Jr., was born. Louis and Viola still frequented Galatoire's and were very much "regulars" . . . they just filled their weekends with grandparenting activities instead.

My beloved father-in-law died in October 1994, at age ninety. Until four days before his death, he was still working three days a week at Phelps Dunbar law firm in downtown New Orleans. There were many loving tributes, letters, and cards to our family when he died—from lawyers, judges, former students at Tulane Law School, and friends. But none touched us more than the beautiful sympathy card we received—signed by every waiter—from Galatoire's.

To the Claveries, dining at Galatoire's is like going home to a much treasured family.

—*Laura Claverie, a New Orleans–based writer and editor and a longtime Galatoire's patron*

Gumbos, Soups, and Stocks

IN OCTOBER 1956, New Orleans writer Shirley Ann Grau recorded in *Holiday* magazine a comment she heard about one of Galatoire's most famous soups: "'Whenever I pass Mr. [Justin] Galatoire on the street, I really don't see him. I just see his turtle soup.' That's a very high compliment indeed." Yes, this is lofty praise, and nearly fifty years after the article was written Galatoire's turtle soup is still considered to be among the finest, if not *the* finest, turtle soup in the city.

Despite New Orleans's sultry climate, hot soups and rich stews are very popular here. After all, the dish for which the city is best known is rich and zesty Creole seafood gumbo. The Galatoire family preserved many of the customs of their French ancestors, including the strong presence of soup on the menu, and many of the restaurant's patrons do not consider dinner to be a complete meal without a soup course.

Most of these soup recipes yield approximately two gallons, enough to feed ten to twelve people. All of them are wonderful just as soon as they come from the pot, but their flavors are all the more enhanced when they are refrigerated overnight and served the next day. Many soups also freeze well and are a welcome find on a cold day.

CORN AND CRAWFISH SOUP

Use only fresh crawfish tails. The sweet flavor from the fat is crucial in the flavoring of the soup, and frozen tails don't work. When prepared properly, the succulent meat of the crawfish plays very pleasantly against the silky sweetness of the corn and the creamy texture of the soup. Add fresh scallions just before serving for a bit of fresh appeal and bright color.

This will keep for two to three days in the refrigerator. Do not freeze.

---

1 POUND SALTED BUTTER

1 BUNCH OF SCALLIONS (GREEN AND WHITE PARTS), SLICED, PLUS ½ CUP ADDITIONAL SLICED SCALLIONS FOR GARNISH

1½ CUPS ALL-PURPOSE FLOUR

12 CUPS CRAWFISH STOCK (PAGE 116)

3 POUNDS FRESH, PEELED LOUISIANA CRAWFISH TAILS

1½ CUPS SWEET CORN, INCLUDING SCRAPINGS FROM THE COB (ABOUT 3 EARS)

2 CUPS HEAVY WHIPPING CREAM

SALT AND FRESHLY GROUND BLACK PEPPER TO TASTE

Melt the butter in a very large stockpot over medium heat. Add the scallions and sauté for 2 minutes, or until they wilt. Add the flour to the butter mixture and whisk for 3 minutes to make a blond roux.

Do not allow the roux to brown. Add the stock to the roux and stir to thoroughly incorporate. Raise the temperature to high and cook for 8 to 10 minutes, bringing the mixture to a simmer. Add the crawfish and corn. Cook for 5 to 6 minutes, until the mixture simmers again. Add the cream and cook the soup for an additional 5 minutes, or until it thickens slightly. Adjust the seasonings with salt and pepper. Serve the soup in individual soup plates. Garnish with scallions.

MAKES 1½ GALLONS; SERVES 10 TO 12

CRAWFISH BISQUE

This version of Galatoire's famous crawfish bisque does not include stuffed crawfish heads, which make the preparation of the dish very time-consuming and labor-intensive to prepare. Instead we have used fresh Louisiana crawfish tails, which are added at the very end of the cooking process.

This will keep for two to three days in the refrigerator. Do not freeze.

---

2 TABLESPOONS VEGETABLE OIL

1 LARGE ONION, FINELY DICED (ABOUT 2 CUPS)

ONE 6-OUNCE CAN TOMATO PASTE

½ CUP ALL-PURPOSE FLOUR

2 CUPS HEAVY WHIPPING CREAM

1 TABLESPOON FINELY MINCED GARLIC

2 GALLONS CRAWFISH STOCK (PAGE 116)

1½ CUPS BRANDY

4 POUNDS FRESH, PEELED LOUISIANA CRAWFISH TAILS

SALT AND CAYENNE PEPPER TO TASTE

Place a large stockpot over high heat and add the vegetable oil. Add the onions and sauté, stirring occasionally, for 6 to 8 minutes, until the onions are caramelized. Add the tomato paste and flour and stir until incorporated. Lower the heat to medium and cook the mixture, stirring continuously, for 5 to 7 minutes, until it becomes brown and sticky. Take extreme care not to burn the mixture. Whisk in the cream and cook for 3 to 4 minutes, whisking constantly, so the mixture will be smooth. Add the garlic and stock and stir to thoroughly incorporate. Bring the mixture to a simmer and cook for 15 minutes, or until it has thickened slightly. Add the brandy and the crawfish tails and cook for an additional 10 minutes. Season with salt and cayenne pepper.

MAKES 2½ GALLONS; SERVES 10 TO 12

JACKSON SOUP

The delicate flavor of the leeks is enhanced when the soup is made a day in advance, chilled, and reheated before serving. A glass of chablis and a hunk of warm, crusty French bread are the perfect accompaniments.

This soup will keep for four days in the refrigerator and a month in the freezer.

SALT TO TASTE

9 LARGE BAKING POTATOES, PEELED AND CUT INTO
    MEDIUM DICE

2 LEEKS, CLEANED AND FINELY DICED (WHITE AND
    GREEN PARTS)

1½ POUNDS SMOKED HAM, CUT INTO MEDIUM DICE

2 CUPS WHOLE MILK

2 CUPS ALL-PURPOSE FLOUR

FRESHLY GROUND WHITE PEPPER TO TASTE

Pour 1½ gallons of water into a stockpot and season with salt. Add the potatoes to the water and bring the mixture to a boil. Reduce the heat to medium and cook the potatoes at a low rolling boil for 5 minutes. Stir in the leeks and ham, and continue at a low rolling boil for 10 minutes, or until the potatoes are soft.

In a mixing bowl, make a cold roux by whisking the milk and flour together until smooth.

Add the cold roux a little at a time to the simmering soup, stirring continuously. Cook over medium heat for about 20 minutes, or until the soup has thickened. Season to taste with salt and white pepper.

MAKES ABOUT 1½ GALLONS; SERVES 8 TO 10

LOBSTER BISQUE

Though lobsters may not be indigenous to southeast Louisiana, this intensely rich, velvety soup is still right at home at Galatoire's.

This will keep for two days in the refrigerator. Do not freeze.

---

3 WHOLE MAINE LOBSTERS (ABOUT 1¼ POUNDS EACH)

2 CUPS VEGETABLE OIL

2 CUPS ALL-PURPOSE FLOUR

3 TABLESPOONS SALTED BUTTER

1 MEDIUM YELLOW ONION, DICED (ABOUT 1 CUP)

½ CELERY STALK, DICED (ABOUT ¼ CUP)

ONE 6-OUNCE CAN TOMATO PASTE

3 TABLESPOONS SALT, PLUS ADDITIONAL TO TASTE

2 TABLESPOONS CAYENNE PEPPER

1 QUART HEAVY WHIPPING CREAM

1 CUP BRANDY

FRESHLY GROUND WHITE PEPPER TO TASTE

Place a large stockpot over high heat. Add 2 gallons of cold water, then add the lobsters. Bring the lobsters to a boil and cook for 7 minutes. Remove the lobsters and set aside. Reserve the cooking water.

Place a heavy sauté pan over high heat and add the oil and flour. Whisk until smooth and cook for 4 to 5 minutes to make a blond roux. Do not allow the roux to brown. Set aside.

Remove the heads from the lobsters, extract the meat from the shells, and set the meat aside. Reserve the shells. Remove the matter from the lobster heads and discard, reserving the cleaned heads. In a 2-gallon pot, melt the butter and sauté the onions, celery, tomato paste, and lobster shells for 3 to 4 minutes. Pour the reserved lobster water into the pot, and then add the 3 tablespoons salt and the cayenne pepper. Bring the mixture to a low rolling boil and cook for 10 minutes. Strain the mixture into another large pot, saving the remaining solids. Discard the lobster shells and purée the vegetables in a food processor or food mill, and add them back to the strained stock. Stir the cream into the mixture, and then bring it back to a low rolling boil. Add ½ cup of the brandy and simmer for 2 minutes, or until very slightly thickened.

Add the roux to the stock gradually, whisking until the soup is smooth and velvety. Dice the lobster meat and add it to the bisque. Adjust the seasoning with salt and white pepper. If desired, add the remaining ½ cup brandy. Serve at once.

MAKES 1½ GALLONS; SERVES 10 TO 12

OYSTER ARTICHOKE SOUP

Unlike most recipes for this favorite regional soup, this one does not include cream or milk. The flavor is light and herbaceous, making it a delightful choice at any time of year.

The oyster liquor is the key to this dish. It'll probably be necessary to have a local oyster or seafood house track this item down for you. Do this in advance when ordering the oysters.

This will keep for two days in the refrigerator or for a month in the freezer.

1½ POUNDS SALTED BUTTER	3 CUPS ALL-PURPOSE FLOUR
1 CUP DICED SCALLIONS (WHITE AND GREEN PARTS)	1½ GALLONS OYSTER LIQUOR
¼ CUP FRESH THYME LEAVES	12 FRESH ARTICHOKE BOTTOMS, COARSELY CHOPPED
¼ CUP SALT	30 OYSTERS
1½ TABLESPOONS FRESHLY GROUND BLACK PEPPER	5 BAY LEAVES

In a large stockpot over high heat, melt the butter. Add the scallions, thyme, salt, and pepper and cook for 3 minutes, or until the scallions are wilted. Whisk in the flour and cook for 2 to 3 minutes, stirring constantly. Add 6 cups of the oyster liquor to the mixture, whisking until the liquid is incorporated. Add the remaining 18 cups oyster liquor gradually, and then cook the mixture for 20 minutes at a low rolling boil. Add the artichokes, oysters, and bay leaves and simmer for 10 minutes more. Correct the seasoning with salt and pepper and discard the bay leaves. Serve the soup hot with warm French bread.

MAKES 1½ GALLONS; SERVES 8 TO 10

Galatoire's

CREOLE SEAFOOD GUMBO

Galatoire's French Creole seafood gumbo is a rich, classic version of New Orleans's most definitive soup. While filé powder, which is often used as a thickening agent, is just fine, we prefer okra in our kitchen.

It's important to remember the secret to a good gumbo: a rich, dark roux. It is a crucial flavoring agent and provides structure for the entire dish.

This will keep for two days in the refrigerator or one month in the freezer.

---

2 CUPS PLUS 3 TABLESPOONS VEGETABLE OIL

1 LARGE ONION, DICED (ABOUT 2 CUPS)

2 CELERY STALKS, SLICED (ABOUT 1 CUP)

TWO 8-OUNCE CANS CRUSHED TOMATOES

2 POUNDS OKRA, STEMMED

1 TABLESPOON SALT

1 TABLESPOON CAYENNE PEPPER

1 TABLESPOON FRESHLY GROUND WHITE PEPPER

3 BAY LEAVES

1½ GALLONS GUMBO CRAB STOCK (PAGE 115)

2 POUNDS MEDIUM (40–50 COUNT) SHRIMP, PEELED

30 OYSTERS

1 POUND JUMBO LUMP CRABMEAT, CLEANED

4 CUPS ALL-PURPOSE FLOUR

2 CUPS STEAMED WHITE RICE

Heat 3 tablespoons of the oil in a stockpot, then add the onions and celery. Sauté over medium-high heat for 5 minutes, or until they are tender and the onions begin to brown.

Add the tomatoes and okra and simmer until the moisture has cooked out. Season with the salt, peppers, and bay leaves and add the stock. Bring to a boil over high heat. Lower the heat to a simmer and add the shrimp, oysters, and crabmeat to the stock. Simmer for 10 minutes.

While the gumbo is simmering, make a roux in a cast-iron or other heavy frying pan: Place the pan over medium heat, and then add the remaining 2 cups of oil and the flour to the pan, whisking until smooth. Continue to cook, whisking constantly, until the roux becomes a walnut color. If the pan starts to get too hot during the cooking process, remove it from the heat, still whisking, and allow it to cool briefly. Be extremely careful not to burn the roux. Constant whisking will keep the roux from sticking.

Stir the brown roux into the soup a little at a time. When all of the roux has been incorporated, simmer the soup for about 10 minutes, until thickened. Remove the bay leaves.

Ladle the gumbo into soup plates or gumbo bowls and garnish with a large spoonful of rice.

MAKES 2 GALLONS; SERVES 10 TO 12

SHRIMP AND EGGPLANT SOUP

Nearly everyone is surprised to learn that there is no cream in this soup. The deceptively creamy texture is imparted by the eggplant, which literally melts away during the cooking process, leaving behind a hearty broth that balances beautifully with the delicate flavor of the small, sweet shrimp.

This will keep for two days in the refrigerator or one month in the freezer.

---

1 POUND SALTED BUTTER

1 SMALL YELLOW ONION, DICED (ABOUT 1 CUP)

1 LARGE EGGPLANT, PEELED AND DICED (ABOUT 5 CUPS)

2 LARGE TOMATOES, DICED AND DRAINED (ABOUT 3 CUPS)

1½ CUPS ALL-PURPOSE FLOUR

1 GALLON SHRIMP STOCK (PAGE 117)

1½ POUNDS SMALL (50–60 COUNT) SHRIMP, PEELED

SALT AND FRESHLY GROUND WHITE PEPPER TO TASTE

Melt the butter in a stockpot over medium heat. Once the butter is melted, increase the heat to medium-high and add the onions, eggplant, and tomatoes. Sauté the vegetables for about 15 minutes, until the onions become caramelized. Whisk the flour into the mixture to make a roux. Reduce the heat to medium and cook for about 2 minutes, stirring. Slowly add the shrimp stock, whisking constantly. Bring the soup to a low rolling boil and cook for 20 minutes. Add the shrimp, reduce the heat to medium-low, and simmer for 10 minutes. Season with salt and pepper.

MAKES 1½ GALLONS; SERVES 8 TO 10

SPLIT PEA SOUP

Straining the soup imparts a smooth, elegant texture that is in keeping with the upscale dining experience at Galatoire's. However, forgoing the straining process will produce a less formal, more country-style version of the classic soup. In this case remove the ham hocks, pull the meat from the bones, and add it back to the soup before serving.

This will keep for four days in the refrigerator or one month in the freezer.

3 POUNDS DRY SPLIT PEAS

2 ONIONS, COARSELY CHOPPED

4 CELERY STALKS, QUARTERED

4 SMOKED HAM HOCKS

SALT AND FRESHLY GROUND BLACK PEPPER TO TASTE

Wash and sort the peas, then place them in a stockpot with 2 gallons of water. Add the onions, celery, and ham hocks. Bring the mixture to a boil over high heat, then reduce the heat to medium-high and cook at a low rolling boil for about 45 minutes, until the peas become soft and begin to dissolve.

Strain the soup through a fine-mesh strainer into another pot. Use a ladle to push down on the solids in the strainer to force all of the liquids and any soft solids through. The majority of the soft solids will be stuck to the underside of the strainer. Remove them with a rubber spatula and add them to the strained soup. These will help thicken the soup. Discard the solid remnants. Season the soup with salt and pepper. Simmer for 5 minutes, or until slightly thickened. Serve at once.

MAKES 1½ GALLONS; SERVES 8 TO 10

SPINACH AND OYSTER SOUP WITH HERBSAINT

This rich soup is particularly appropriate for holiday season entertaining, when oysters are at their prime. Despite its deep, lush flavors, it is relatively quick and easy to prepare. If your oysters, when drained, do not yield enough liquor for the recipe, add enough cold water to the oyster liquor to make one gallon, put the oysters back into the liquor–water mixture, refrigerate for at least one hour, then drain the oysters, reserve the liquid, and proceed with the recipe.

This soup will keep for three days in the refrigerator or one month in the freezer.

5 TABLESPOONS SALTED BUTTER	1 TEASPOON CHOPPED GARLIC
1 CUP YELLOW ONION, FINELY DICED	1 QUART HEAVY WHIPPING CREAM
1 CUP ALL-PURPOSE FLOUR	2 PINTS OYSTERS
1 GALLON OYSTER LIQUOR	1 POUND FRESH SPINACH, COARSELY CHOPPED
3 BAY LEAVES	1 CUP HERBSAINT LIQUEUR
3 SPRIGS OF FRESH THYME	SALT AND FRESHLY GROUND WHITE PEPPER TO TASTE

In a stockpot over medium-high heat, melt the butter. Add the onions and cook for 5 to 7 minutes, until they are translucent. Stir the flour into the butter and cook for 2 to 3 minutes, until the mixture is bubbling at the edges. Add the oyster liquor, bay leaves, and thyme. Cook the mixture at a low rolling boil for 20 minutes, skimming off any foam that collects on the surface.

Add the garlic and cream, and bring the mixture back to a low boil. Cook the soup for 20 minutes, and then add the oysters, spinach, and Herbsaint. Adjust the seasoning with salt and white pepper. Simmer for about 5 minutes, or until the oysters are firm. Remove the bay leaves and thyme sprigs before serving.

MAKES ABOUT 1½ GALLONS; SERVES 8 TO 10

Turtle Soup au Sherry

Though many visitors to New Orleans are surprised to find it, most of the city's Creole restaurants serve turtle soup, and New Orleanians take great delight in arguing over who serves the best. Galatoire's has used the same recipe since the restaurant opened in 1905, and, if its popularity is any indication, it ranks among the very finest.

When serving this soup to guests, present it with a small cruet of dry sherry and allow them to adjust the flavor to their preference.

---

1 LARGE YELLOW ONION, QUARTERED

2 CELERY STALKS, COARSELY CHOPPED

3 GREEN BELL PEPPERS, SEEDED AND COARSELY CHOPPED

1½ POUNDS TURTLE MEAT (HAVE YOUR BUTCHER GRIND IT)

1 GALLON VEAL STOCK (SEE PAGE 267; THE STOCK IS ACHIEVED BY FOLLOWING THE VEAL DEMI-GLACE RECIPE BUT EXCLUDING THE FINAL REDUCTION STEP)

ONE 8-OUNCE CAN CRUSHED TOMATOES

¼ CUP SPANISH HOT PAPRIKA

3 TABLESPOONS SALT

1½ TEASPOONS CHOPPED FRESH THYME LEAVES

1 LEMON, SEEDED AND CUT INTO 8 PIECES

2 LARGE HARD-BOILED EGGS, COARSELY CHOPPED

1 CUP DRY SHERRY

½ CUP FINELY CHOPPED CURLY PARSLEY

2 CUPS VEGETABLE OIL

2 CUPS ALL-PURPOSE FLOUR

Begin by putting the onions, celery, and bell peppers into a food processor, and process until minced. Sauté the turtle meat and minced vegetables for 5 to 7 minutes, until all of the turtle meat is browned. Add the stock, tomatoes, paprika, salt, and thyme. Bring to a boil and reduce the heat to medium. Simmer the soup for 40 minutes. Add the lemons, eggs, sherry, and parsley and simmer for 30 minutes, skimming off any foam that collects on the surface of the soup.

While the soup is cooking, make a roux. Add the oil to a heavy sauté pan over medium heat. Whisk in the flour and begin cooking the roux. Whisk continuously, until it turns light brown. Add the roux to the soup slowly, taking care that the soup does not boil over. Simmer for another 5 minutes after the roux has been incorporated. Serve immediately.

Makes 1½ gallons; serves 8 to 10

GALATOIRE'S GOES TO THE DOGS: CANINE CARNIVAL ROYALTY TOAST
THE BEGINNING OF THEIR OFFICIAL REIGN AT GALATOIRE'S

On February 13, 2004, Galatoire's became the official meeting place for the King and Queen of the Mystic Krewe of Barkus, the world's first all-canine Carnival krewe. King Barkus XII, Manouche Marino, toasted his queen, Holly Bell, over Friday lunch, heralding their official reign over the 2004 Canine Carnival season.

King Manouche, "a very strange, cosmetically challenged mix of something like a Pomeranian and a Terrier," had been found roaming around Bourbon Street years earlier by Tony and Patty Marino of New Orleans. Queen Holly, also a pavement pounder in a previous life, was rescued from the brink of death by Ms. Ann Bell, also of New Orleans. Her Majesty Queen Holly wore her six-foot black velvet queen's cape for the official meeting with her consort.

An annual tradition was established at Galatoire's, when, on January 27, 2005, King Barkus XIII, Bee Bop Coleman, toasted his queen, Honey Gelderman, over lunch, as they began their official reign over the 2005 Canine Carnival season.

King Bee Bop, a Cavalier King Charles Blenheim spaniel born in Ireland, is the son of Mr. and Mrs. James Coleman, Jr. Although His Majesty Barkus XIII frequently jets about the globe, it was his first Galatoire's luncheon. He toasted his commoner queen with grace and a sniff.

Queen Honey, the daughter of Mr. and Mrs. Tony Gelderman, has no idea where she was born and was once homeless. However, her life on the streets quickly changed when she was found and adopted into the Gelderman family. Queen Honey is following in the footsteps of her human mother, Katherine Gelderman, who reigned as the Queen of Carnival (Krewe of Rex) in 1982.

"We are honored that Galatoire's has become the official meeting place for these distinguished dignitaries," said Michele Galatoire. "We provide them with the same impeccable service all of our guests expect."

Gumbo Crab Stock

"Gumbo crabs" are skinnier, less desirable crabs that wouldn't get used for their meat. They are sold with the back shell already removed to allow the stock or gumbo liquid access to the meat and fat within, resulting in delicious flavor. This stock can be made up to one day in advance. Freeze it if you need to keep it longer. It will last for one month in the freezer.

5 GUMBO CRABS (BOUGHT FROZEN)

2 CELERY STALKS, COARSELY CHOPPED

1 LARGE ONION, COARSELY CHOPPED

2 BAY LEAVES

2 LEMONS, HALVED

12 BLACK PEPPERCORNS, CRUSHED

Combine the crabs, celery, onions, bay leaves, lemons, and peppercorns in a large stockpot with 2½ gallons of water. Bring to a boil and reduce to a simmer. Simmer for 45 minutes. Strain the stock and discard the solids.

MAKES 2 GALLONS

CRAWFISH STOCK

Making crawfish stock is not for the weak at heart. If putting live creatures over an open fire makes you squeamish, have someone else do this for you. It is best to make this stock shortly before you will need it. This stock will keep, refrigerated, for one day. It will keep for one month in the freezer.

1 LARGE ONION, DICED (ABOUT 2 CUPS)

4 CELERY STALKS, DICED (ABOUT 2 CUPS)

ONE 6-OUNCE CAN TOMATO PASTE

2 BAY LEAVES

3 POUNDS LIVE CRAWFISH

Place a large stockpot over medium heat. Add the onions, celery, tomato paste, and bay leaves and sauté for 8 to 10 minutes, stirring continuously, until the mixture is a rusty light brown color. Add the crawfish and stir, folding the whole crawfish through the mixture. If some of the crawfish are mashed in the process the quality of the stock will improve. Cook the mixture for 4 to 5 minutes, until all of the shells have turned bright red. Add 2½ gallons of water to deglaze the pot. Increase the heat to high and bring to a rolling boil. Once a rolling boil is achieved, reduce the heat until you obtain a low boil and cook the stock for 45 minutes. Strain the stock through a wire mesh strainer and discard the solids.

MAKES 2 GALLONS

SHRIMP STOCK

This stock will hold in the refrigerator for two to three days and in the freezer for one month.

2 POUNDS FRESH SHRIMP SHELLS AND HEADS

1 LARGE ONION, HALVED

2 CELERY STALKS, COARSELY CHOPPED

2 BAY LEAVES

10 BLACK PEPPERCORNS, CRUSHED

1 LEMON, HALVED

Place all of the ingredients in a large stockpot with 1 gallon of cold water. Bring the mixture to a boil, skimming any foam as necessary. Reduce the heat to a low boil and cook for 45 minutes. Strain the stock and discard the solids.

MAKES 2 QUARTS

FISH STOCK

This stock will keep in the refrigerator for two to three days and in the freezer for one month.

2 POUNDS FISH BONES

1 LARGE ONION, HALVED

2 CELERY STALKS, COARSELY CHOPPED

2 BAY LEAVES

10 BLACK PEPPERCORNS, CRUSHED

1 LEMON, HALVED

Remove the fish heads from the skeletons and rinse all thoroughly under cold running water to remove any traces of blood. Place all of the ingredients in a large stockpot with 1 gallon of cold water. Bring the mixture to a boil, skimming any foam as necessary. Reduce the heat to a low boil and cook for 45 minutes. Strain the stock and discard the solids.

MAKES 2 QUARTS

Omelettes and Eggs

AMERICANS GENERALLY ASSOCIATE EGGS with breakfast. But for New Orleans's early Creoles, breakfast was not as other Americans know it today. The city's hard-working inhabitants began their days early with cups of strong, hot coffee before they set about their tasks. By mid-morning they were famished and repaired to the table for a breakfast (*le petit déjeuner*) of gargantuan proportions. The meals customarily started with soup and progressed to a seafood course, a meat course, a salad, and, finally, dessert. In addition to coffee and tea, light white wine was a common breakfast beverage.

In European fashion, egg dishes were popular choices for all meals of the day in New Orleans 100 years ago and, therefore, they were and still are offered at all times of the day at Galatoire's, typically as entrées.

CREOLE OMELETTE

The Creole Sauce is a delicious filler for this simple, classic omelette.

3 LARGE EGGS	SALT AND FRESHLY GROUND BLACK PEPPER TO TASTE
1 TABLESPOON SALTED BUTTER	¼ CUP CREOLE SAUCE (PAGE 256)

In a small bowl, beat the eggs with a whisk until well blended and fluffy.

In an 8-inch nonstick sauté pan over high heat, melt the butter. Pour the eggs into the pan and stir with a rubber spatula until the eggs begin to firm up. Season with salt and pepper and allow the omelette to cook without stirring for about 1 minute, until the bottom is golden brown and the top is almost set. Using a spatula, loosen the edges of the omelette, then flip the omelette over and cook the top for a few seconds.

Slide the omelette onto a plate, add the Creole sauce, and fold the omelette in half over the sauce. Serve at once.

MAKES 1 LARGE OMELETTE THAT WILL SERVE 1 TO 2

ASPARAGUS OMELETTE

The ingredients in this omelette reflect classic French cooking. It was first introduced to the menu by Jean Galatoire himself, who probably carried the recipe with him from his homeland near Pau, France. The asparagus lends a delicate, slightly herbaceous quality, which counters pleasantly with the potent Gruyère cheese. For a truly decadent brunch, add two ounces of jumbo lump crabmeat to the pan when you sauté the asparagus.

3 LARGE EGGS

1 TABLESPOON SALTED BUTTER

¼ CUP COOKED ASPARAGUS

SALT AND FRESHLY GROUND BLACK PEPPER TO TASTE

¼ CUP SHREDDED GRUYÈRE CHEESE (OPTIONAL)

In a small bowl, beat the eggs with a whisk until well blended and fluffy.

In an 8-inch nonstick sauté pan over medium-high heat, melt the butter. Add the asparagus and cook for 1 to 2 minutes, until thoroughly heated through. Pour the eggs into the pan and stir with a rubber spatula until the eggs begin to firm up. Season with salt and pepper and allow the omelette to cook without stirring for about 1 minute, until the bottom is golden brown and the top is almost set. Using a spatula, loosen the edges of the omelette, then flip the omelette over and cook the top for a few seconds.

Slide the omelette onto a plate and top with the cheese, if desired. Fold the omelette in half and serve immediately.

MAKES 1 LARGE OMELETTE THAT WILL SERVE 1 TO 2

BACON AND MUSHROOM OMELETTE

This recipe makes an impressive creation from common ingredients most of us have in the refrigerator.

3 LARGE EGGS

2 TABLESPOONS SALTED BUTTER

¼ CUP SLICED BUTTON MUSHROOMS

¼ CUP COARSELY CHOPPED COOKED BACON (FROM ABOUT 3 SLICES)

SALT AND FRESHLY GROUND BLACK PEPPER TO TASTE

¼ CUP SHREDDED CHEDDAR CHEESE (OPTIONAL)

In a small bowl, beat the eggs with a whisk until well blended and fluffy.

In an 8-inch nonstick sauté pan over high heat, melt the butter. Sauté the mushrooms for 2 minutes, or until softened. Add the bacon to the eggs and mix well. Pour the eggs into the pan and stir with a rubber spatula until the eggs begin to firm up. Season with salt and pepper and allow the omelette to cook without stirring for about 1 minute, until the bottom is golden brown and the top is almost set. Using a spatula, loosen the edges of the omelette, then flip the omelette over and cook the top for a few seconds.

Slide the omelette onto a plate and top with the cheese, if desired. Fold the omelette in half and serve immediately.

MAKES 1 LARGE OMELETTE THAT WILL SERVE 1 TO 2

CRABMEAT OMELETTE

This dish is absolutely beautiful in its simplicity. Use only the very freshest ingredients. There is no place for a substandard ingredient to hide here.

3 LARGE EGGS

1 TABLESPOON SALTED BUTTER

2 TABLESPOONS FINELY CHOPPED SCALLIONS (WHITE AND GREEN PARTS)

3 OUNCES JUMBO LUMP CRABMEAT, CLEANED

SALT AND FRESHLY GROUND BLACK PEPPER TO TASTE

In a small bowl, beat the eggs with a whisk until well blended and fluffy.

In an 8-inch nonstick sauté pan over high heat, melt the butter. Sauté the scallions for 2 minutes, or until wilted. Add the crabmeat and sauté for an additional minute until the crabmeat is just heated through. Pour the eggs into the pan and stir with a rubber spatula until the eggs begin to firm up. Season with salt and pepper and allow the omelette to cook without stirring for about 1 minute, until the bottom is golden brown and the top is almost set. Using a spatula, loosen the edges of the omelette, then flip the omelette over and cook the top for a few seconds.

Slide the omelette onto a plate and fold it in half. Serve at once.

MAKES 1 LARGE OMELETTE THAT WILL SERVE 1 TO 2

SAUTÉED OYSTER OMELETTE

The addition of sautéed oysters gives this omelette a mild briny flavor that is pleasantly offset by the scallions and the rich butter.

---

3 LARGE EGGS

1 TABLESPOON SALTED BUTTER

6 RAW OYSTERS, COARSELY CHOPPED

2 TABLESPOONS FINELY CHOPPED SCALLIONS (WHITE AND GREEN PARTS)

SALT AND FRESHLY GROUND BLACK PEPPER TO TASTE

In a small bowl, beat the eggs with a whisk until well blended and fluffy.

In an 8-inch nonstick sauté pan over high heat, melt the butter. Add the oysters and the scallions and sauté for 1 minute, or until the edges of the oysters begin to curl and the scallions are tender. Pour the eggs into the pan and stir with a rubber spatula until the eggs begin to firm up. Season with salt and pepper and allow the omelette to cook without stirring for about 1 minute, until the bottom is golden brown and the top is almost set. Using a spatula, loosen the edges of the omelette, then flip the omelette over and cook the top for a few seconds.

Slide the omelette onto a plate and fold in half. Serve at once.

MAKES 1 LARGE OMELETTE THAT WILL SERVE 1 TO 2

GALATOIRE'S FAMILY OF WAITERS

The elegant environment of Galatoire's has served as a welcoming beacon to no fewer than seven members of the same extended Cajun family from Ville Platte, Louisiana. "There are four of us Fontenots—Harold, Billy, John, and Homer; two Sylvesters–Dorris and Bryant; and a LaFleur—Louis," said Billy, age thirty-eight. "All of us are related: the Fontenots and the Sylvesters by blood, LaFleur by marriage."

Billy's father, Harold Fontenot, age sixty-eight, was lured to New Orleans by the appeal of working in one of the city's famous restaurants, instead of entering his family's sweet potato and cotton farming business. Harold left his hometown in 1953 and took a job at Arnaud's restaurant. He moved over to Galatoire's in 1962 or '63—"can't remember," he said. He's been a fixture in the dining room ever since.

"I've never even considered leaving," Harold continued. "I feel like I'm a part of this place."

So much a part, in fact, that Billy considered a position at the restaurant a "natural choice" while he worked on his accounting degree at University of New Orleans. Billy worked as an accountant for a while but soon realized he preferred the restaurant lifestyle more. "It's a good life," Billy said. "It feels right here." In May 2005, Billy celebrated sixteen years from the day he first joined the restaurant.

"It's the customers that I would miss the most," Billy said. "You really get to know them, know their habits. They show up and you put their drink on the table and their order in the kitchen. You just know what makes them happy. Those are the locals but I've also met exciting people from all over the world."

And so the dining room buzzes with that rare brand of camaraderie, good humor, and warmth only a bunch of hearty Cajuns could impart to an environment such as Galatoire's. John Fontenot plays it up, calling everyone "cher," the Cajun term of endearment, and delighting the masses with his boundless good humor. Dorris Sylvester, age seventy-three, is a quiet source of security and comfort to the customers who have called on him since he arrived from the Roosevelt Hotel some thirty years ago.

Like everyone on the Galatoire's staff, the family members know one another's habits. They cover the bases when a coworker is overwhelmed.

"It's just not like other places," said Bryant Sylvester, age forty-two. "In other places people just go their separate ways. Here, the front of the house is tight-knit. We look out for one another— not just those of us who are blood, but all of us."

SAUTÉED SHRIMP OMELETTE

The combination of shrimp and garlic makes this a potent omelette that is as appropriate for dinner as for breakfast. Serve it with a green salad and a chilled chablis in true French (and French Creole) fashion.

---

3 LARGE EGGS

1 TABLESPOON SALTED BUTTER

6 UNCOOKED LARGE (21–25 COUNT) SHRIMP, PEELED
    AND DICED, OR ⅓ CUP SMALL SHRIMP

1 TEASPOON CHOPPED GARLIC

SALT AND FRESHLY GROUND BLACK PEPPER TO TASTE

In a small bowl, beat the eggs with a whisk until well blended and fluffy.

In an 8-inch nonstick sauté pan over high heat, melt the butter. Add the shrimp and sauté for 3 minutes, or until they turn pink. Add the garlic and sauté for an additional minute. Pour the eggs into the pan and stir with a rubber spatula until the eggs begin to firm up. Season with salt and pepper and allow the omelette to cook without stirring for about 1 minute, until the bottom is golden brown and the top is almost set. Using a spatula, loosen the edges of the omelette, then flip the omelette over and cook the top for a few seconds.

Slide the omelette onto a plate and fold in half. Serve at once.

MAKES 1 LARGE OMELETTE THAT WILL SERVE 1 TO 2

HAM AND CHEESE OMELETTE

A popular favorite at both French and American tables for breakfast, lunch, or a light dinner.

---

3 LARGE EGGS

1 TABLESPOON SALTED BUTTER

¼ CUP DICED HAM

SALT AND FRESHLY GROUND BLACK PEPPER TO TASTE

¼ CUP SHREDDED CHEDDAR CHEESE

In a small bowl, beat the eggs with a whisk until well blended and fluffy.

In an 8-inch nonstick sauté pan over high heat, melt the butter. Add the ham and sauté for 2 minutes, until heated through. Pour the eggs into the pan and stir with a rubber spatula until the eggs begin to firm up. Season with salt and pepper and allow the omelette to cook without stirring for about 1 minute, until the bottom is golden brown and the top is almost set. Using a spatula, loosen the edges of the omelette, then flip the omelette over and cook the top for a few seconds.

Slide the omelette onto a plate, add the cheese, and fold the omelette in half over the cheese. Serve at once.

MAKES 1 LARGE OMELETTE THAT WILL SERVE 1 TO 2

EGGS BENEDICT

Some version of this classic dish can be found on most New Orleans brunch menus, and Galatoire's is no exception. This hearty combination of poached eggs and ham is served under a blanket of the buttery hollandaise sauce for which we are famous. It is one of our most popular dishes for Sunday brunch. Many Galatoire's patrons enjoy Eggs Benedict with Creole Bloody Marys (page 27), Milk Punch (page 30), or chilled champagne.

1 CUP RED WINE VINEGAR

12 LARGE EGGS

6 English muffins cut in half and spread with
    BUTTER

12 PIECES OF HAM ¼ INCH THICK, CUT TO THE SIZE AND
    SHAPE OF AN ENGLISH MUFFIN

2 CUPS HOLLANDAISE SAUCE (PAGE 249)

Preheat the broiler on low.

Combine 1 gallon of water and the red wine vinegar in a large sauté pan and bring to a simmer over medium heat. Poach the eggs in 2 batches of 6 eggs: Crack the eggs one at a time over the surface of the water, and then let the egg drop gently into the liquid. Use a slotted spoon to pull any white streamers back to the egg. Cook the eggs for 3 to 4 minutes, occasionally pushing them with a slotted spoon to keep them from sticking together, until the whites are firm but the yolks are still soft. Be careful not to overcook the eggs. When the eggs are done, remove them from the water with a slotted spoon and pat dry. Repeat the process with the remaining 6 eggs.

While the eggs are poaching, place the buttered muffin halves and the ham on a cookie sheet. Place under the broiler for 4 minutes, or until the muffins are golden and crisp and the ham is heated through.

Place 2 broiled English muffin halves with ham on each of 6 plates. Place the poached eggs on top of the ham. Finish the dish by spooning hollandaise sauce atop the eggs, allowing it to pool onto the ham and muffin.

SERVES 6

EGGS SARDOU

Galatoire's French Quarter neighbor, Antoine's restaurant, first created a version of this dish, which has become a classic New Orleans brunch entrée. The tangy lemon flavors in the hollandaise play beautifully against the creamed spinach. Galatoire's cooks and cleans an average of 200 artichoke bottoms each day for use in this dish as well as for Crabmeat Sardou (page 156) and Crabmeat Yvonne (page 160), all of which are among our best sellers.

JUICE OF 2 LEMONS

12 ARTICHOKES

1 CUP RED WINE VINEGAR

12 LARGE EGGS

1 RECIPE CREAMED SPINACH (PAGE 214)

1 RECIPE HOLLANDAISE SAUCE (PAGE 249)

Bring 3 quarts of water and the lemon juice to a boil in a large saucepan. Trim ½ inch from the top of each artichoke and remove as many of the outside leaves as possible. Place the trimmed artichokes in the boiling water; reduce the heat and simmer, covered, for about 25 minutes, until the bottoms are tender and the leaves are easy to remove. Cool the artichokes until they can be easily handled. Remove all of the leaves and the fuzzy interior choke. Trim the bottoms of the artichokes so they sit flat. Set aside.

Bring 1 gallon of water and the vinegar to a low boil in a large saucepan. Poach the eggs in 2 batches of 6 eggs: Crack the eggs one at a time over the surface of the water, and then let the egg drop gently into the liquid. Use a slotted spoon to pull any white streamers back to the egg. Cook the eggs for 3 to 4 minutes, occasionally pushing them with a slotted spoon so they do not stick together, until the whites are firm but the yolks are still soft. Be careful not to overcook the eggs. When the eggs are done, remove them from the water with a slotted spoon and pat dry. Repeat the process with the remaining 6 eggs.

Spoon about ⅔ cup of creamed spinach onto the centers of 6 plates. Remove the artichoke bottoms from the water, drain briefly, pat dry, and place 2 bottoms on each bed of spinach. Nestle an egg into each artichoke bottom and blanket the eggs with hollandaise sauce. Serve at once.

SERVES 6

Fish and Shellfish Entrées

NEW ORLEANS IS BLESSED with a natural abundance of large shrimp, briny oysters, plump crabs, sweet crawfish, and dozens of varieties of succulent fish that pour forth from the Mississippi Sound, Lake Pontchartrain, area bayous, and the Gulf of Mexico. On the Galatoire's table you'll find redfish, snapper, speckled trout, lemonfish (cobia), tuna, and pompano.

"I can recall when the Catholic Church said it was okay to eat meat on Fridays—except during Lent," said Chris Ansel, Jr., grandson of Justin Galatoire. "I remember talking to Battistella, the fishmonger, on the phone and he was panicked that sales of fish and seafood would plummet. What actually happened was that the demand for fish went way up because people were no longer forced to eat it."

Many consider seafood to be Galatoire's specialty. The restaurant offers an extensive array of dishes that celebrate the region's natural aquatic bounty.

BROILED POMPANO WITH MEUNIÈRE BUTTER

This is the simplest possible dish to prepare—once you are lucky enough to find the pompano. It may seem too simple, even . . . but it is truly all about the fish. The oily flesh of the pompano has incredible flavor and this preparation allows it to stand alone without distraction. If you are unable to find pompano, consider another member of the jack family, which includes amberjack.

SIX 10-OUNCE POMPANO FILLETS WITH SKIN ON (THREE 1¾-POUND POMPANO, SPLIT IN HALF; DISCARD BONE)

1 CUP CLARIFIED BUTTER (PAGE 248)

SALT AND FRESHLY GROUND BLACK PEPPER TO TASTE

1½ CUPS MEUNIÈRE BUTTER (PAGE 263)

3 LEMONS, CUT INTO WEDGES

Preheat the broiler on the low setting.

Lay the pompano fillets flat in a heavy pan, flesh side up. Brush the fillets with clarified butter and season them with salt and pepper. Broil the fish for 6 minutes, or until golden brown. Remove from the broiler.

Plate the pompano and nap ¼ cup of meunière butter atop each fillet. Serve with lemon wedges.

SERVES 6

GRILLED LEMON FISH WITH SAUTÉED JUMBO LUMP CRABMEAT

Absolute simplicity is common in Galatoire's kitchen. So much of the restaurant's magic, particularly with regard to seafood, stems from the superior quality of the raw ingredients. This simplicity means the dishes are easy for the home cook to prepare. The tricky part is that there is simply nowhere to hide a flaw in dishes as transparent as this one. Purchase only the very freshest fish available from a reputable fishmonger or catch it and cook it yourself.

3 TABLESPOONS SALTED BUTTER

1 POUND JUMBO LUMP CRABMEAT

SALT AND FRESHLY GROUND BLACK PEPPER TO TASTE

SIX 8-OUNCE LEMON FISH (COBIA) FILLETS, ABOUT
    ½ INCH THICK, OR ANOTHER FIRM, FLAKY WHITE
    FISH, SUCH AS RED OR BLACK DRUM

¼ CUP OLIVE OIL

1 RECIPE MEUNIÈRE BUTTER (PAGE 263)

3 LEMONS, CUT INTO WEDGES

Preheat an outdoor gas or charcoal grill.

In a medium sauté pan, melt the butter over medium-high heat. Add the crabmeat and season with salt and pepper. Stir very gently and sauté for 4 minutes, or until heated through. Set aside while grilling the fish.

Brush the fish fillets with olive oil and season with salt and pepper. Grill the fish for 3 minutes on each side, taking care not to overcook. Remove from the grill.

Immediately place the lemon fish fillets in the centers of 6 dinner plates. If the crabmeat has become cold, flash-heat it over high heat and equally divide it atop the 6 fish fillets. Drizzle meunière butter atop each dish and garnish with lemon wedges. Serve at once.

SERVES 6

Note: If you are using an alternate type of fish you may have to adjust the cooking time.

Grilled Salmon with Poached Oysters and Shallot Cream

Spinach, cream, and Herbsaint are mainstays in the Galatoire's kitchen. For this dish they were brought together in a fresh new manner, with results we are proud of. The rich nature of the salmon, offset by the equally rich cream sauce, dictates that other courses of the meal should be kept on the light side. Begin the meal with a fresh salad and finish with an assortment of macerated fresh fruits.

---

2 TABLESPOONS SALTED BUTTER

2 LARGE SHALLOTS, FINELY DICED

¼ CUP FINELY DICED FENNEL (STEMS AND BULB)

¼ CUP HERBSAINT LIQUEUR

2 CUPS HEAVY CREAM

18 LARGE GULF OYSTERS, SHUCKED

¼ POUND (ABOUT 2½ CUPS) FRESH SPINACH, CLEANED AND STEMMED

6 SALMON FILLETS (8 OUNCES EACH)

¼ CUP OLIVE OIL

SALT AND FRESHLY GROUND BLACK PEPPER TO TASTE

Preheat an outdoor gas or charcoal grill.

In a medium sauté pan over high heat, melt the butter. Add the shallots and fennel and sauté for 4 to 5 minutes, until they begin to caramelize. Add the Herbsaint and simmer for 1 minute to deglaze the pan. Add the cream. Bring the mixture to a simmer, reduce the heat to medium, and simmer for 5 minutes, or until the sauce has thickened slightly. Add the oysters and the spinach. Stir to incorporate the ingredients and remove from the heat. The spinach will wilt and the edges of the oysters will curl slightly from the residual heat in the pan. Set aside and keep warm while grilling the salmon.

Coat the salmon fillets on both sides with the olive oil and season with salt and pepper. Place the salmon into a grilling basket and place the basket on the hot grill. Cook for 4 minutes, then carefully turn the fillets and grill the other side for an additional 4 minutes.

Equally divide the shallot cream, including the spinach leaves, across 6 plates. Place the salmon fillets atop the cream and spinach leaves. Garnish each plate by placing 3 poached oysters around the salmon fillets. Serve at once.

SERVES 6

GRILLED REDFISH WITH SAUTÉED GULF SHRIMP

When Cajun cooking became extremely popular in the mid-1980s the demand for redfish was so great as to have threatened the survival of the species. Commercial procurement of the fish was outlawed and restaurants were practically forbidden to sell it. It was a dark time in New Orleans's culinary history.

Thankfully, those troubled days have passed and we are now free once again to enjoy this firm, low-fat, flavorful fish that lends itself equally well to broiling, baking, stuffing, grilling, and frying.

---

4 TABLESPOONS (½ STICK) SALTED BUTTER

30 LARGE (21–25 COUNT) GULF SHRIMP, PEELED

¼ CUP FINELY CHOPPED SCALLIONS (WHITE AND GREEN PARTS)

SALT AND FRESHLY GROUND BLACK PEPPER TO TASTE

SIX 8-OUNCE REDFISH FILLETS, SKIN AND SCALES INTACT

¼ CUP OLIVE OIL

1 RECIPE MEUNIÈRE BUTTER (PAGE 263)

3 LEMONS, CUT INTO WEDGES

Preheat an outdoor gas or charcoal grill.

Melt the butter in a medium sauté pan. Add the shrimp and sauté for 4 minutes, or until they begin to turn pink. Add the scallions and sauté for an additional 2 minutes, or until tender. Season with salt and pepper. Set aside while you grill the fish.

Brush the fillets with olive oil and season with salt and pepper. Place the redfish flesh side down on the hot grill for 3 minutes, or until the edges are no longer translucent. Turn the fish so the scales are down and continue cooking for an additional 8 minutes, or until the flesh is fully opaque. Remove from the grill.

Immediately place the redfish fillets in the centers of 6 plates. If the shrimp have become cold, flash-heat them in the pan over high heat and equally divide the mixture atop the 6 fish fillets. Drizzle with meunière butter and garnish with lemon wedges. Serve at once.

SERVES 6

Grilled Yellowfin Tuna Steak with Wilted Spinach and Pepper Jelly Glaze

In recent years pepper jelly, long a popular homemade southern condiment enjoyed with cheese, has become more widely enjoyed as a cooking glaze. Its sweet-hot, though slightly vinegary, quality enables it to balance hearty varieties of meat, game, and fish. We have found that it pairs particularly well with yellowfin tuna, a firmly textured, flaky, and tender fish with a moderate to high fat content.

In addition, the vibrant green of the wilted spinach beautifully offsets the light ruby hue of the tuna's interior, making it a feast for the eyes.

One 10-ounce jar pepper jelly

4 tablespoons (½ stick) salted butter

1 tablespoon minced garlic

2 pounds cleaned and stemmed fresh spinach leaves

Salt and freshly ground black pepper to taste

Six 8-ounce yellowfin tuna steaks (each about 1 inch thick)

¼ cup olive oil

Preheat an outdoor gas or charcoal grill.

Melt the pepper jelly in a small pan over low heat. Keep warm while preparing the spinach and tuna.

Melt the butter in a large sauté pan over high heat. Add the garlic and the spinach and sauté for 1 minute, or until the leaves have wilted. Season with salt and pepper. Set the spinach aside while grilling the tuna.

Brush each side of the tuna with olive oil and season with salt and pepper. Place the tuna steaks on the hot grill and cook for 1½ minutes. Turn the steaks by a quarter turn to create a diamond pattern of grill marks on the tuna. Cook for an additional 1½ minutes. Turn the steaks over and grill for an additional 3 minutes, or until the exterior is very lightly browned. Take care not to overcook the tuna. It should be served medium-rare with a warm pinkish-red center.

Divide the wilted spinach equally among 6 plates and spread it into a thin bed for the tuna steak to sit atop that will still allow the vibrant color of the spinach to be seen. Place the tuna steaks onto the beds of wilted spinach and drizzle over the warm melted pepper jelly.

Serves 6

POACHED SHEEPSHEAD WITH HOLLANDAISE SAUCE

This elegant dish was popular from the time Galatoire's opened until the middle of the last century, when poached fish fell out of fashion. The sheepshead, indisputably one of the sea's ugliest creatures, makes up for its less-than-beautiful exterior with a firm, flavorful, snow-white flesh that holds up admirably to the poaching process. A light gloss of lemony hollandaise is all that is needed as embellishment.

½ CUP RED WINE VINEGAR

2 BAY LEAVES

1 SMALL ONION, COARSELY CHOPPED

1 CELERY STALK, COARSELY CHOPPED

SIX 8-OUNCE SHEEPSHEAD FILLETS (YOU CAN ALSO
    SUBSTITUTE BLACK DRUM, REDFISH, OR HALIBUT)

1 RECIPE HOLLANDAISE SAUCE (PAGE 249)

3 LEMONS, CUT INTO WEDGES, FOR GARNISH

1 BUNCH OF WATERCRESS, FOR GARNISH

In a medium saucepan, heat 2 quarts of water with the vinegar, bay leaves, onions, and celery and bring to a low simmer over medium heat. Add the sheepshead fillets, reduce the heat to medium-low, and poach for 10 to 12 minutes, until cooked through.

Make the hollandaise sauce while the fish is poaching and set it aside.

Remove the poached sheepshead fillets from the water with a slotted spatula and pat dry with a paper towel. Discard the cooking liquid and the vegetables.

Place the poached fillets at the centers of 6 dinner plates. Nap the hollandaise in perpendicular lines across the fillets, allowing it to puddle slightly on each side of the fish. Garnish with lemon wedges and sprigs of watercress.

SERVES 6

POACHED TROUT MARGUERY

The original Parisian version of this dish called for fillet of sole and its sauce contained fresh mussels and truffles. Finding none of those ingredients in New Orleans, Galatoire's founder, Jean Galatoire, adapted the famed dish of his French homeland using ingredients indigenous to Louisiana. This version, a classic at Galatoire's, has been offered at the restaurant since the very beginning.

---

1 CUP BÉCHAMEL SAUCE (PAGE 251)

1 RECIPE HOLLANDAISE SAUCE (PAGE 249)

½ CUP RED WINE VINEGAR

SIX 5-OUNCE TROUT FILLETS

3 TABLESPOONS SALTED BUTTER

2 DOZEN LARGE (21–25 COUNT) SHRIMP, PEELED AND COARSELY CHOPPED

2 CUPS SLICED BUTTON MUSHROOMS

SALT AND FRESHLY GROUND BLACK PEPPER TO TASTE

Keep the béchamel and hollandaise sauces warm while you prepare the fish.

In a medium saucepan, heat 2 quarts of water and the red wine vinegar to a low simmer.

Line a work surface with plastic wrap and place the trout fillets side by side atop the plastic wrap. Place another piece of plastic wrap atop the fillets. Gently pound the trout with a meat mallet, taking care not to tear the fillets. When the trout is uniformly flat, gently remove the plastic wrap. Begin on the tail end of the fillet and roll each fillet jelly-roll style. Fasten with toothpicks.

Submerge the trout in the simmering water and vinegar. Allow the trout to simmer for 9 to 10 minutes, until it is cooked through and opaque.

Make the sauce while the fish is poaching: Melt the butter in a large sauté pan. Add the shrimp and sauté over high heat for 3 minutes, or until the shrimp turn pink. Stir frequently to avoid sticking. Add the mushrooms and season with salt and pepper. Sauté for an additional 2 minutes, or until the mushrooms are soft. Add the béchamel sauce to the pan and reduce the heat to low. Just before you remove the poached trout from the water, remove the shrimp and mushroom mixture from the heat and stir in the hollandaise sauce. Set the sauce aside.

Remove the trout from the water with a slotted spoon and pat dry with paper towels. Remove the toothpicks and center the poached pieces of trout on 6 plates. Equally divide the shrimp sauce atop the poached fish and serve immediately.

SERVES 6

POMPANO EN PAPILLOTE

The elegant pompano is a saltwater delicacy best known to the south Atlantic and Gulf states. This fine fish is rarely seen on restaurant menus but it is a frequent treat for Galatoire's diners. Galatoire's has spent many years nurturing relationships with those fishermen who will provide the restaurant with the plumpest, most desirable pompano available.

This version of pompano en papillote utilizes some of Louisiana's most prized indigenous ingredients, including shrimp and oysters.

Serve this dish when you want to make a dramatic impression. Do not open the parchment packets until everyone is assembled at the table. When the packets are cut open and the fragrant steam escapes you are sure to hear applause.

---

1 CUP RED WINE VINEGAR

JUICE OF 1 LEMON

SIX 8- TO 10-OUNCE FILLETS OF POMPANO, SKINNED, RIB BONES REMOVED

6 TABLESPOONS SALTED BUTTER

1 CUP SLICED BUTTON MUSHROOMS

5 FINELY CHOPPED SCALLIONS (GREEN AND WHITE PARTS), ABOUT 1/2 CUP

1 TABLESPOON FRESH THYME LEAVES

2 TABLESPOONS MINCED GARLIC

1/4 CUP ALL-PURPOSE FLOUR

1/2 CUP WHITE WINE

2 CUPS OYSTER LIQUOR

1/2 CUP HEAVY CREAM

18 LARGE (21–25 COUNT) SHRIMP, PEELED

18 LARGE OYSTERS, SHUCKED

1 TEASPOON SALT

1 TEASPOON FRESHLY GROUND WHITE PEPPER

1 CUP CLARIFIED BUTTER (PAGE 248)

Preheat the oven to 375°F.

To a large sauté pan over high heat add 2 quarts water and the vinegar and lemon juice and bring the mixture to a simmer. Submerge the pompano in the simmering mixture and poach for 10 minutes. Remove the fish from the water to a platter lined with paper towels. Carefully remove and discard any pin bones from the fish. Set the fish aside.

In a large sauté pan over high heat, melt the salted butter. Add the mushrooms and scallions and sauté for 3 minutes, or until tender. Add the thyme and garlic and remove the pan from the heat. Whisk in the flour to create a roux. Add the white wine and oyster liquor to the roux and whisk the ingredients to fully incorporate. Return the pan to the heat and bring the mixture to a simmer over high heat. Cook for 5 minutes, reduce the heat to medium, and add the cream. Bring to a simmer again and cook for an additional 5 minutes, or until the mixture begins to thicken. Add the shrimp and oysters and simmer for an additional 5 minutes, or until the shrimp have turned pink and the edges of the oysters have begun to curl. Remove the pan from the heat. Season with the salt and pepper.

Cut 6 sheets of parchment paper about 15 × 24 inches each. Trim each sheet into a heart shape with a crease down the middle. Place a large spoonful of sauce onto each piece of paper, and then top each with a pompano fillet, 3 shrimp, and 3 oysters. Divide the remaining sauce among the 6 portions. Fold the paper over the contents. Starting at the bottom corner of the paper and working around the edge, seal the packet by making small overlapping creases. Carefully transfer the packets to baking sheets and brush the paper with clarified butter. Bake for 5 minutes, or until the parchment has turned brown and puffed up. Depending on the size of your oven it may be necessary to bake the packets in two or even three batches.

Place the pouches onto dinner plates. Using scissors, carefully cut the top of each pouch in a half circle around the edge near the crease. Fold the flap over and serve at once.

Serves 6

POTATO-CRUSTED BLACK DRUM WITH THYME BEURRE BLANC

The potato crusting process takes time, but it is worth every bit of effort. The coating seals in the juices from the fish and allows it to steam in the crust, which turns crispy and crunchy.

Serve this dish with simple steamed asparagus or haricots verts and a glass of light, fruity white wine, such as Viognier.

---

2 LARGE IDAHO POTATOES, PEELED

¼ CUP TABASCO SAUCE

JUICE OF 5 LEMONS

1 TABLESPOON SALT, PLUS ADDITIONAL TO TASTE

1 TEASPOON FRESHLY GROUND WHITE PEPPER

SIX 8-OUNCE BLACK DRUM FILLETS, OR OTHER FIRM,
    FLAKY FISH

FRESHLY GROUND BLACK PEPPER TO TASTE

1 CUP ALL-PURPOSE FLOUR

1 CUP CLARIFIED BUTTER (PAGE 248)

1 RECIPE THYME BEURRE BLANC (PAGE 266)

6 THYME SPRIGS, FOR GARNISH

3 LEMONS, CUT INTO WEDGES

Preheat the oven to 350°F.

Rinse the potatoes and shred them using a cheese grater or the shredding disk of a food processor. This will yield about 3 cups of potatoes. Toss the shredded potatoes in a large mixing bowl with the Tabasco, lemon juice, 1 tablespoon salt, and white pepper. Set aside.

Clear a large work space. Season the fish with salt and black pepper. Divide the shredded potatoes in half. Create 6 equal portions of shredded potato from half of the mixture. Squeeze excess liquid from the portioned potatoes and lay out the 6 portions of potatoes on a sheet of parchment paper. Shape each portion to the shape of the drum fillets. Dust the fish fillets with flour and place each atop a portion of shredded potatoes. Divide the remaining half of the potatoes into 6 equal portions and squeeze each to remove excess liquid. Place a portion atop each drum fillet. Spread the potatoes so they cover the fillets.

Divide the clarified butter between 2 large ovenproof sauté pans or cast-iron skillets. Place the pans over high heat. When the pans are very hot and a drop of water vaporizes on contact, use a large spatula or fish turner to move the fish and shredded potatoes from the parchment paper to the hot pans. Once each pan has 3 fillets in it, reduce the heat to medium and sauté for 3 to 5 minutes, allowing the shredded potatoes and flour to bind and the potatoes to turn golden brown and crispy. Turn the fish. Remove the pans from the heat and place them into the preheated oven. Bake for 10 minutes.

Make the thyme beurre blanc while the fish is in the oven.

Center a potato-crusted fillet on a dinner plate. Nap the thyme beurre blanc across the fish, allowing it to pool on the plate. Take care not to completely cover the golden potato crust. Adorn the fish with a thyme sprig and a wedge of lemon.

SERVES 6

REDFISH COURT BOUILLON

Court bouillon *literally means a "short boil." New Orleanians make this classic French poaching method all their own with redfish "coo-bee-yawn." While steamed rice is the classic accompaniment, some local families have been known to serve the redfish, vegetables, and flavorful broth ladled atop mashed potatoes in shallow soup bowls.*

2 LARGE TOMATOES

2 TABLESPOONS UNSALTED BUTTER

2 GREEN BELL PEPPERS, JULIENNED (ABOUT 2 CUPS)

1 LARGE ONION, JULIENNED (ABOUT 2 CUPS)

2 TEASPOONS MINCED GARLIC

1 CUP DRY WHITE WINE

6 REDFISH FILLETS (8 OUNCES EACH), OR OTHER FIRM, FLAKY FISH

3 TEASPOONS SALT

1 TEASPOON FRESHLY GROUND BLACK PEPPER

2 TEASPOONS CAYENNE PEPPER

3 CUPS STEAMED RICE

Bring 1 quart of water to a boil in a medium saucepan. Blanch the tomatoes in the water for about 1 minute, just until the skin breaks. Remove the hot tomatoes from the water and drain. Let them cool for 10 minutes, then pull off the skin. Seed and julienne the tomatoes and set them aside.

Melt the butter in a large sauté pan over high heat. Sauté the bell peppers and onions for 3 minutes, or until tender. Add the tomatoes and garlic and sauté for an additional 3 minutes. Deglaze the pan with the wine and simmer the wine and vegetables for 1 minute, then add 1 quart of water to make the court bouillon.

Season the fish with the salt and black and cayenne peppers and submerge in the court bouillon. Bring the mixture to a boil, then reduce the temperature to medium-high and simmer for 12 minutes, or until the fish is cooked and opaque.

Place a small mound of rice at the top of 6 plates. Remove the redfish from the broth and put a piece on each plate. Evenly distribute the vegetables and broth atop the redfish fillets.

SERVES 6

SAUTÉED BLACK DRUM WITH CRABMEAT YVONNE

Here we have paired fresh, flaky Gulf drum with our decadent, versatile Crabmeat Yvonne garnish. While jumbo lump crabmeat is rather costly, the dish is simple and quick to prepare, making it an impressive, yet manageable, choice for entertaining. As the dish includes fresh artichoke it would be a particularly lovely choice for an Easter or early spring dinner.

To save time when preparing this dish for entertaining, you may prepare the artichokes up to one day ahead.

---

1 RECIPE CRABMEAT YVONNE (PAGE 161)

6 BONELESS BLACK DRUM FILLETS (8 TO 10 OUNCES
    EACH), OR OTHER FLAKY WHITE FISH

SALT AND FRESHLY GROUND BLACK PEPPER TO TASTE

2 CUPS ALL-PURPOSE FLOUR

2 CUPS CLARIFIED BUTTER (PAGE 248)

LEMON WEDGES, FOR GARNISH (OPTIONAL)

Prepare the crabmeat Yvonne and set aside.

Season the fish with salt and pepper and dust with the flour. Cover the bottom of a large sauté pan with the clarified butter and set over medium-high heat. Shake any excess flour from the fish and sauté for 4 to 5 minutes per side, until a golden brown crust is formed.

If the crabmeat mixture has cooled, briefly reheat it over high heat. Place each fish fillet on a warmed plate. Distribute the crabmeat mixture evenly atop each fillet. Garnish with lemon wedges, if desired. Serve at once.

SERVES 6

Trout Meunière Amandine

Meunière, *French for "miller's wife," refers to a style of cooking whereby a food, often fish, is seasoned, lightly dusted with flour, and simply sautéed. The final product is served with* beurre meunière, *a brown butter flavored with lemon. This quintessential Creole dish blends two classic French presentations—* meunière *and* amandine *("garnished with almonds")—with fine speckled trout from the waters of the Gulf of Mexico. This is our most popular entrée. The contrast of the soft, succulent texture of the fish, the light tartness of the lemon–butter sauce, and the sweet crunch of toasted almonds is pretty irresistible. The dish is also easy to make at home.*

---

3 CUPS SLICED ALMONDS

2 LARGE EGGS

1 PINT WHOLE MILK

SALT AND FRESHLY GROUND BLACK PEPPER TO TASTE

6 SPECKLED TROUT FILLETS (7 TO 8 OUNCES EACH),
    CLEANED AND BONED

2 CUPS ALL-PURPOSE FLOUR

1 GALLON VEGETABLE OIL

1 RECIPE MEUNIÈRE BUTTER (PAGE 263)

3 MEDIUM LEMONS, CUT INTO WEDGES

Preheat the oven to 300°F.

Place the almonds in a pan and toast them in the oven for 15 to 20 minutes, opening the oven to stir them every 5 minutes while they cook. When they become a light golden brown, remove from the oven and set aside.

Make a wash by whisking the eggs and the milk. Season with salt and pepper. Season the trout fillets with salt and pepper and dust with flour. Submerge the floured trout in the egg wash. Gently remove the fillets from the egg wash and allow the excess to drip off. Put the fillets back into the flour, then gently shake off the excess flour.

In a large, heavy-bottomed pot, heat the oil to 350°F. Test the readiness of the oil by sprinkling a pinch of flour over it. The flour will brown instantly when the oil has reached the correct temperature. Add the trout and fry for 4 to 5 minutes. Remove the fish when the crust is golden brown.

Top each fried trout fillet with almonds and warmed meunière butter. Garnish with lemon wedges and serve at once.

SERVES 6

CRABMEAT SARDOU

The verdant creamy spinach, lumps of white crabmeat, and golden hollandaise sauce make this dish as visually appealing as it is delicious. Though it is available at any time, Crabmeat Sardou (a very exciting variation on Eggs Sardou) is immensely popular with Galatoire's Sunday brunch crowd. If their preferences are an accurate indication, this dish is particularly good when washed down with generous amounts of champagne and peals of laughter.

12 ARTICHOKES	1 RECIPE CREAMED SPINACH (PAGE 214)
JUICE OF 1 LEMON	½ CUP CLARIFIED BUTTER (PAGE 248)
1 RECIPE HOLLANDAISE SAUCE (PAGE 249)	2 POUNDS JUMBO LUMP CRABMEAT, CLEANED

In a large pot, submerge the artichokes in water, add the lemon juice, and boil for approximately 30 minutes, or until the stems are tender. Allow the artichokes to cool and peel all of the exterior leaves from the artichoke hearts. Using a spoon or your thumb, remove and discard the chokes, leaving only the bottoms. Cut the excess stems off the bottoms so they sit flat.

While waiting for the artichokes to cook and cool, prepare the hollandaise sauce and the creamed spinach. Set aside.

Add the clarified butter to a medium sauté pan over medium heat. Add the crabmeat and stir, taking care not to break the lumps. Sauté for 3 minutes, or until the crabmeat is heated through. Remove from the heat.

Spoon equal portions of the creamed spinach onto 6 dinner plates. Place 2 artichoke bottoms into each bed of spinach. Remove the crabmeat from the pan with a slotted spoon in order to drain excess butter. Discard the excess butter. Divide the crabmeat into equal portions and place it into the cavities of the artichoke bottoms. Top the crabmeat with a generous portion of hollandaise sauce. Serve immediately.

SERVES 6

CRABMEAT AU GRATIN

The use of gratin dishes is essential to the success of this recipe. The shallow dishes are either round or oval and allow for a great deal of surface area to be exposed to the heat from the broiler, ensuring a golden crispy topping for each portion.

Rich as this is, a simple green salad with vinaigrette and French bread complete the meal.

---

2 TABLESPOONS SALTED BUTTER

¼ CUP FINELY CHOPPED SCALLIONS (WHITE AND GREEN PARTS)

1 POUND JUMBO LUMP CRABMEAT, CLEANED

1 CUP BÉCHAMEL SAUCE (PAGE 251)

½ CUP SHREDDED MILD CHEDDAR CHEESE

½ CUP DRIED BREAD CRUMBS

½ CUP CLARIFIED BUTTER (PAGE 248)

Preheat a broiler on low.

In a large sauté pan over high heat, melt the butter. Add the scallions and sauté for 2 minutes, or until tender. Add the crabmeat and sauté for an additional 3 minutes, or until the crabmeat is heated through. Reduce the heat to low and gently fold in the Béchamel sauce and cheese, taking care not to break the lumps of crabmeat. Remove from the heat once the cheese is melted.

Spoon the mixture into 4 large gratin dishes. Sprinkle the tops with the bread crumbs and drizzle with the clarified butter, coating the bread crumbs. Place under the broiler until golden brown and serve immediately.

SERVES 4

CRABMEAT RAVIGOTE

This classic New Orleans dish has long been a standard for gracious local hostesses, and it is an especial favorite during the holiday season, when everyone is ready to indulge. Crabmeat Ravigote can be served in individual ramekins or gratin dishes or placed in a chafing dish for buffet-style entertaining. The canapés should be passed at the table or presented alongside the dish.

The canapés can be made the day before and stored in a sealed container at room temperature.

ONE 16-INCH FRENCH BAGUETTE, SLICED IN ¼-INCH-THICK ROUNDS

½ CUP CLARIFIED BUTTER (PAGE 248)

2 TABLESPOONS SALTED BUTTER

¼ CUP FINELY CHOPPED SCALLIONS (WHITE AND GREEN PARTS)

1 POUND JUMBO LUMP CRABMEAT, CLEANED

1 TEASPOON SALT

½ TEASPOON CAYENNE PEPPER

1 CUP BÉCHAMEL SAUCE (PAGE 251)

1 CUP HOLLANDAISE SAUCE (PAGE 249)

Preheat the oven to 250°F.

Brush the bread rounds with the clarified butter and bake on a cookie sheet for 10 minutes, or until golden brown and crispy. Set the canapés aside.

Melt the salted butter in a large sauté pan over medium-high heat. Add the scallions and sauté for 2 minutes, or until tender. Add the crabmeat, mix gently, and sauté for an additional 3 minutes, or until the crabmeat is heated through. Add the salt, cayenne, and béchamel sauce. Cook, stirring, for about 2 minutes, just until the mixture is hot, then remove it from the heat and fold in the hollandaise. Adjust the seasoning with additional salt and cayenne pepper, if desired. Serve at once with the canapés.

SERVES 4

CRABMEAT YVONNE

Our Crabmeat Yvonne was named for Yvonne Galatoire Wynne, Justin Galatoire's stately, elegant daughter, who devoted herself to Galatoire's from the late 1930s through 2000, serving as front cashier and later as president of the restaurant. It can be used as a garnish for fish, meat, or poultry or it can be enjoyed on its own, as we suggest here. Crawfish Yvonne is a wonderful alternative (see Variation).

The artichokes can be prepared up to one day in advance, making the dish a breeze to prepare when entertaining.

---

6 FRESH ARTICHOKES

JUICE OF 1 LEMON

1 RECIPE MEUNIÈRE BUTTER (PAGE 263)

1 POUND DOMESTIC BUTTON MUSHROOMS, SLICED

1 BUNCH OF SCALLIONS (WHITE AND GREEN PARTS), CHOPPED

1 POUND JUMBO LUMP CRABMEAT, CLEANED

LEMON QUARTERS, FOR GARNISH (OPTIONAL)

In a large pot, submerge the artichokes in water, add the lemon juice, and boil for approximately 30 minutes until the stems are tender. Allow the artichokes to cool and peel all of the exterior leaves from the artichoke hearts. Using a spoon or your thumb, remove and discard the chokes, leaving only the bottoms. Cut the bottoms into slices. Set aside.

In a large skillet over medium heat, heat the meunière butter. Add the mushrooms, artichokes, and scallions and sauté. Gently fold in the crabmeat and continue to sauté until the crabmeat is heated through. Remove from the heat. Garnish with lemon quarters, if desired. Serve at once.

SERVES 6

Variation: For Crawfish Yvonne, simply substitute 2 pounds of peeled fresh crawfish tails for the crabmeat.

F R I E D   S O F T - S H E L L   C R A B S

There are no substitutes for soft-shell crabs; they are one of the world's great delicacies. The crabs must be harvested during the very brief time when the crustacean has cast off its shell in order to grow one that's larger, leaving it with a soft, edible shell. As brutal as it sounds, the crabs must be purchased alive as close to cooking time as possible. They should be cleaned just moments before they hit the pot.

This recipe affords each diner with a very generous entrée of two whole crabs. Small crabs, known as "busters," can be used for appetizer portions. While the meunière butter is all the adornment needed, many Galatoire's patrons enjoy their soft-shell crabs served "avec meunière amandine." For this variation, simply sprinkle each crab with about one-quarter toasted sliced almonds before adding the meunière butter.

12 LARGE SOFT-SHELL CRABS	3 CUPS ALL-PURPOSE FLOUR
1 GALLON VEGETABLE OIL	1 RECIPE MEUNIÈRE BUTTER (PAGE 263)
4 LARGE EGGS	3 LEMONS, CUT INTO WEDGES
1 QUART WHOLE MILK	

Clean the crabs by paring off the eyes and trimming the tails with kitchen scissors. Gently pull back the shells from the pointed ends and remove the gills underneath on both sides. Lay the shells back flat. Refrigerate the crabs until ready to use.

In a large, heavy-bottomed pot suitable for frying, heat the oil to 350°F.

In a large mixing bowl, whisk the eggs and milk. Place the flour in a separate large mixing bowl. Dust the crabs in the flour, then submerge them in the egg wash. Gently remove the crabs from the wash and allow the excess to drip off. Put the crabs back into the flour once again. Test the readiness of the oil by sprinkling a pinch of flour over it. The flour will brown instantly when the oil has reached the correct temperature. When the oil is ready, gently shake off any excess flour on the crabs and fry them in the hot oil for 4 to 5 minutes, turning halfway through, until they have formed a golden crust. Remove the crabs from the oil with tongs. Place the crabs on a platter lined with paper towels to drain for 2 minutes.

Put 2 crabs on each dinner plate and nap each with warm meunière butter. Garnish with lemon wedges and serve immediately.

SERVES 6

Sautéed Soft-Shell Crabs

This recipe calls for two large crabs per person—a very generous portion. If you are planning a multicourse dinner you might wish to consider serving each person only one crab; otherwise, round out this very abundant entrée with a simple green salad and some chilled white wine.

12 LARGE SOFT-SHELL CRABS	1 RECIPE MEUNIÈRE BUTTER (PAGE 263)
2 CUPS ALL-PURPOSE FLOUR	¼ CUP CHOPPED CURLY PARSLEY, FOR GARNISH
2 CUPS CLARIFIED BUTTER (PAGE 248)	4 LEMONS CUT INTO WEDGES, FOR GARNISH

Clean the crabs by paring off the eyes and trimming the tails with kitchen scissors. Gently pull back the shells from the pointed ends and then remove the gills underneath on both sides. Lay the shells back flat.

Dredge the cleaned crabs in the flour and shake off the excess. The flour will stick to the soft shells. Add the clarified butter to a large sauté pan over high heat. Sauté the crabs for 4 minutes per side, or until golden brown.

Arrange 2 crabs each on 6 dinner plates and drizzle with warm meunière butter. Garnish with chopped parsley and lemon wedges. Serve at once.

SERVES 6

MUSSELS SAINT-PIERRE

Only in recent years have Americans begun to appreciate the fresh mussels that Europeans have favored for centuries. The creamy tan meat of the mussel is slightly firmer than that of oysters and clams but it is also pleasantly sweeter.

When shopping for mussels, choose only those with tightly closed shells or those that snap shut when tapped. If the mussel rattles when shaken it is a sign that it is dead and should be rejected. Also avoid those that feel notably heavier than their counterparts. The shells are probably filled with sand. Smaller mussels will generally be more tender than larger ones.

Our customers also love Crabmeat Saint-Pierre (see Variation). In either case, this recipe produces a generous amount of rich broth that cries out to be served with plenty of warm French bread. Ladle the mussels or crabmeat and broth into a pretty soup tureen, place it at the center of the table, and allow guests to serve themselves family style.

---

2 POUNDS MUSSELS

2 LARGE TOMATOES

2 TABLESPOONS SALTED BUTTER

1 CUP SLICED BUTTON MUSHROOMS

¼ CUP FINELY SLICED SCALLIONS (GREEN AND WHITE PARTS)

2 TABLESPOONS MINCED GARLIC

1 TEASPOON SALT

1 TEASPOON CAYENNE PEPPER

½ CUP DRY WHITE WINE

Scrub the mussels with a brush under cold running water and pull off or cut off the beards. Discard any mussels with cracked or open shells. Set the mussels aside.

Bring 1 quart of water to boil in a medium saucepan. Blanch the tomatoes in the water about 1 minute, just until the skin breaks. Remove the hot tomatoes from the water, drain, and cool for 10 minutes. Pull off the skin, seed and dice the tomatoes, and set them aside.

Melt the butter in a large sauté pan over high heat. Add the mushrooms and sauté for 2 minutes, or until tender. Add the scallions and tomatoes and sauté for 2 to 3 minutes, until the tomatoes begin to stick to the pan. Add the garlic, salt, and cayenne pepper and toss to incorporate. Keep the temperature high as you deglaze the pan with the white wine, and immediately add the mussels. Sauté for 2 minutes. Add 2 cups of water and bring to a simmer. Simmer for 4 to 5 minutes, until the mixture reduces slightly. Serve at once.

SERVES 6

Variation: For Crabmeat Saint-Pierre, substitute 1 pound of jumbo lump crabmeat, picked over, for the mussels, and increase the button mushrooms to 8 ounces (about 2 cups). After deglazing the pan with wine, add the crabmeat and 2 cups of water. Simmer for 10 minutes and serve immediately.

CRAWFISH ETOUFFÉE

Louisiana cooks make this quick, easy favorite in large batches because it is perfect for entertaining and, during crawfish season, it is an inexpensive crowd pleaser. Be sure to make enough so you will have leftovers. It tastes even better the next day.

2 CUPS VEGETABLE OIL

1 LARGE ONION, DICED (ABOUT 2 CUPS)

3 CUPS ALL-PURPOSE FLOUR

1 GALLON CRAWFISH STOCK (PAGE 116)

2 POUNDS FRESH, PEELED LOUISIANA CRAWFISH TAILS
   WITH FAT

2 TEASPOONS FRESHLY GROUND BLACK PEPPER

2 TABLESPOONS SALT

3 TABLESPOONS PAPRIKA

½ TEASPOON CAYENNE PEPPER

1 TABLESPOON MINCED GARLIC

1 BUNCH OF SCALLIONS (GREEN AND WHITE PARTS),
   FINELY CHOPPED (ABOUT ½ CUP)

1 BAY LEAF

3 CUPS STEAMED WHITE RICE

To a large stockpot over medium heat, add the oil. Add the onions and sauté for 3 to 4 minutes, until translucent. Add the flour and whisk until smooth. Cook for 4 to 5 minutes, until the roux is light brown. Add the stock and bring to a simmer.

While the mixture simmers, in a large mixing bowl combine the crawfish tails and their fat, black pepper, salt, paprika, cayenne, and garlic.

When the stock has simmered for 10 minutes, incorporate the seasoned crawfish tails into the pot. Scrape the bowl with a rubber spatula to ensure that none of the seasoning is left behind. Add the scallions and bay leaf and simmer for an additional 20 minutes. Discard the bay leaf and serve the crawfish etouffée with steamed rice.

SERVES 6

Shrimp au Vin

This dish is quick and simple, yet the light, fresh flavor is elegant enough for even the most discerning guests. Once you have the shrimp, the rest of the recipe comes together with ingredients common to most home kitchens.

1½ CUPS (3 STICKS) PLUS 2 TABLESPOONS SALTED
    BUTTER, CUT INTO SMALL PIECES

½ CUP FINELY CHOPPED SCALLIONS (WHITE AND GREEN
    PARTS)

2 CUPS SLICED BUTTON MUSHROOMS

4 DOZEN LARGE (21–25 COUNT) SHRIMP, PEELED

1 TABLESPOON MINCED GARLIC

½ TEASPOON CAYENNE PEPPER

1½ CUPS DRY WHITE WINE

2 CUPS STEAMED WHITE RICE

¼ CUP CHOPPED CURLY PARSLEY, FOR GARNISH

Melt 2 tablespoons of the butter in a large sauté pan over high heat. Add the scallions and mushrooms and sauté for 2 to 3 minutes, until the vegetables are tender. Add the shrimp, garlic, and cayenne and sauté for 3 to 4 minutes, until the shrimp turn pink and begin to stick to the pan. Deglaze the pan with the white wine. Cook the mixture for 5 to 7 minutes, until the liquid is reduced by half. Add the remaining butter a few pieces at a time, whisking constantly until all of the butter is incorporated into the sauce.

Using a ramekin or small cup, mold ½-cup portions of rice onto each of 4 dinner plates. Equally distribute the shrimp and sauce around the rice and garnish with the parsley. Serve at once.

SERVES 4

FRIED LOUISIANA GULF SHRIMP

Fried shrimp are as familiar to Louisiana's children (particularly on Fridays and during Lent) as hamburgers are to youngsters elsewhere. Avoid the temptation to dress up your presentation of fried shrimp. Simply remove them from the cooking oil, drain them on paper towels or brown paper (paper grocery bags work well), and serve them with Tartar Sauce (page 265), lemon wedges, and ketchup.

To make a shrimp po-boy sandwich, slice a piece of French bread lengthwise and toast (if desired). Add the condiments of your choice (mayonnaise, Creole mustard, hot sauce, ketchup, tartar sauce), and the "dressings" of your choice (lettuce, tomato, pickle). Then pile on the fried shrimp and enjoy. Ice-cold beer is the perfect accompaniment.

---

1 GALLON VEGETABLE OIL

6 DOZEN LARGE (21–25 COUNT) SHRIMP

4 LARGE EGGS

1 QUART WHOLE MILK

3 CUPS ALL-PURPOSE FLOUR

3 CUPS YELLOW CORN FLOUR

SALT AND FRESHLY GROUND BLACK PEPPER TO TASTE

3 LEMONS, CUT INTO WEDGES

In a large, heavy-bottomed pot suitable for frying, heat the oil to 350°F.

Peel the shrimp, except for the tail section. Devein the shrimp, cutting them so they are partially butterflied.

Whisk the eggs and milk in a large mixing bowl. Add the all-purpose flour to a second large mixing bowl and the yellow corn flour to a third bowl. Season the shrimp with salt and pepper and dust in the all-purpose flour. Submerge the floured shrimp in the egg wash. Remove the shrimp from the egg wash gently and allow the excess to drip off. Put the shrimp into the corn flour. Test the readiness of the oil by sprinkling a pinch of flour over it. The flour will brown instantly when the oil is the correct temperature. When the oil is ready, gently shake off the excess flour from the shrimp and fry in the oil for 3 to 4 minutes, until golden. Remove the shrimp from the oil with a large slotted spoon or metal skimmer. Place the shrimp on a platter lined with paper towels to drain. Serve hot, garnished with lemon wedges.

SERVES 6

SHRIMP CLEMENCEAU

This unusual combination is an absolute favorite among Galatoire's patrons, many of whom enjoy it with a crisp white wine such as Pouilly Fuissé. Do not attempt to "dress up" the dish by using fresh or frozen green peas instead of the canned petit pois called for here. The fancy stuff simply does not work. Stick to the easy way.

OIL, FOR FRYING

3 BAKING POTATOES (ABOUT 10 OUNCES EACH), PEELED AND CUT INTO ¾-INCH SQUARES

SALT AND FRESHLY GROUND BLACK PEPPER TO TASTE

3 TABLESPOONS SALTED BUTTER

6 DOZEN LARGE (21–25 COUNT) SHRIMP, PEELED

3 CUPS SLICED BUTTON MUSHROOMS

3 TABLESPOONS MINCED GARLIC

2 CUPS CANNED PEAS (PETIT POIS)

In a heavy-bottomed pot suitable for frying, heat the oil to 350°F.

Fry the potatoes in 2 batches, moving the pieces around with a slotted spoon to ensure even browning. Cook for 7 to 9 minutes, until golden brown. Remove the potatoes from the oil with a slotted spoon to a platter lined with paper towels. Sprinkle with salt and pepper and set the potatoes aside in a warm place.

Melt the butter in a large sauté pan over high heat. Sauté the shrimp for 3 to 4 minutes, until they turn pink. Add the mushrooms and sauté for an additional 2 to 3 minutes, until they are tender. Add the garlic and the peas and sauté for 2 to 3 minutes, until the peas are thoroughly heated. Season with salt and pepper. Add the potatoes to the pan and toss to incorporate.

Equally distribute the shrimp Clemenceau among 6 plates and serve immediately.

SERVES 6

SHRIMP CREOLE

Creole cuisine is an amalgamation of French, Spanish, and African cuisines with an emphasis on butter and cream. It is a more refined cooking style than Cajun cooking, which uses rendered pork fat as a browning medium over other fats. Creole cooking also incorporates more tomatoes whereas Cajun cooking relies more on potent spices for flavor. Both cooking styles utilize chopped green bell peppers, onions, and celery—the "holy trinity"—as aromatics.

4 LARGE TOMATOES	2 TEASPOONS SALT
2 TABLESPOONS SALTED BUTTER	½ TEASPOON CAYENNE PEPPER (OR MORE TO TASTE)
1 CELERY STALK, CHOPPED (ABOUT ½ CUP)	1 TEASPOON HOT PAPRIKA
1 CUP DICED GREEN BELL PEPPER (ABOUT 1 SMALL)	3 CUPS SHRIMP STOCK (PAGE 117)
1½ CUPS DICED ONION (ABOUT 1 LARGE)	6 DOZEN LARGE (21–25 COUNT) SHRIMP, PEELED
¼ CUP TOMATO PASTE	3 CUPS STEAMED WHITE RICE
1 BAY LEAF	¼ CUP CHOPPED CURLY PARSLEY, FOR GARNISH

Bring 1 quart of water to a boil in a medium saucepan. Blanch the tomatoes in the water about 1 minute, just until the skin breaks. Remove the hot tomatoes from the water and drain. Allow them to cool for 10 minutes, then pull off the skin. Seed and dice the tomatoes, then set them aside.

Melt the butter in a large pot over high heat. Add the celery, bell peppers, onions, and tomatoes and sauté for 7 to 10 minutes, until the tomatoes are nearly dissolved and the vegetables begin to caramelize. Reduce the heat to medium and add the tomato paste, bay leaf, salt, cayenne, and paprika. Allow the mixture to simmer for an additional 3 to 4 minutes, until the vegetables are a rich caramel color. Add the shrimp stock and simmer the mixture at a low rolling boil over medium heat for 25 minutes, or until it is slightly thickened. Add the shrimp and simmer for an additional 10 minutes, or until they are pink and cooked through. Discard the beay leaf.

Place ½ cup of steamed rice in the center of 6 large-rimmed soup plates. Surround the rice with the shrimp and spoon all of the additional sauce over the shrimp. Garnish with the chopped parsley. Serve at once.

SERVES 6

SHRIMP MARGUERY

This unctuous, satisfying dish must be served immediately after preparation. Invite enough guests to ensure there are no leftovers. It cannot be successfully reheated. The sauce separates and the shrimp become undesirably rubbery. What a terrible waste of such a fantastic dish.

---

3 TABLESPOONS SALTED BUTTER	SALT AND FRESHLY GROUND BLACK PEPPER TO TASTE
4 DOZEN LARGE (21–25 COUNT) SHRIMP, PEELED	1 CUP BÉCHAMEL SAUCE (PAGE 251)
3 CUPS SLICED BUTTON MUSHROOMS	1 RECIPE HOLLANDAISE SAUCE (PAGE 249)

Melt the butter in a large sauté pan. Add the shrimp and sauté over high heat for 3 minutes, or until the shrimp turn pink. Add the mushrooms and season with salt and pepper. Sauté for an additional 2 minutes, or until the mushrooms are soft. Add the béchamel sauce to the pan and reduce the heat to low. Simmer for 3 minutes, or until heated through. Remove the pan from the heat and stir in the hollandaise sauce.

Distribute the shrimp and sauce equally among 4 gratin or small casserole dishes and serve immediately.

SERVES 4

GALATOIRE'S SEAFOOD STUFFED EGGPLANT

The steamed flesh of the eggplant is simmered with shrimp and lumps of crabmeat before it is gently folded with béchamel sauce and the dish is broiled—making for a surprisingly light and airy final result. This dish works equally well as an entrée or side dish.

As an alternative for a large holiday gathering, omit the eggplant "shells" and bake the stuffing in a lightly buttered glass baking dish. It is a sensational accompaniment to meat, game, and poultry as well as other seafood preparations, such as whole baked fish.

The dish can be assembled a day ahead, refrigerated, and brought to room temperature before the final broiling.

---

2 LARGE EGGPLANTS

1 TABLESPOON OLIVE OIL

SALT AND FRESHLY GROUND WHITE PEPPER TO TASTE

½ CUP SEASONED DRIED BREAD CRUMBS

¼ CUP PARMESAN CHEESE

½ CUP CLARIFIED BUTTER (PAGE 248)

¼ CUP FINELY CHOPPED SCALLIONS (WHITE AND GREEN PARTS)

¼ CUP FINELY CHOPPED CURLY PARSLEY

2 DOZEN LARGE (21–25 COUNT) SHRIMP, BOILED, PEELED, AND COARSELY CHOPPED

1 POUND JUMBO LUMP CRABMEAT, CLEANED

CAYENNE PEPPER TO TASTE

1 RECIPE BÉCHAMEL SAUCE (PAGE 251)

Preheat either an indoor grill or a broiler on the low setting.

Cut the stems and ends off the eggplants. Peel one of the eggplants and cut into 1-inch cubes. Slice the other eggplant lengthwise into 6 pieces about ¼ to ½ inch thick. Cut a thin slice on both sides to remove the peel. If there is any pulp remaining in the second eggplant, peel it and chop it as well. Steam the 1-inch eggplant cubes in a steamer basket until soft.

Brush the 6 strips of eggplant with olive oil, season with salt and white pepper, and grill or broil until tender and golden. Set the cooked pieces aside until it is time to put the stuffing on them.

Blend the bread crumbs and the Parmesan in a small bowl. Set aside.

Heat the clarified butter in a large sauté pan over medium-high heat. Add the scallions and parsley and sauté for 1 minute, or until wilted. Add the shrimp, crabmeat, and steamed eggplant pulp, and season the mixture with salt, white pepper, and cayenne pepper. Sauté for another 3 to

4 minutes over medium heat. Fold in the béchamel sauce and half of the bread crumb–cheese mixture and allow the stuffing to simmer for 1 minute for all of the ingredients to marry.

Preheat a broiler on the low setting.

Divide the stuffing into 6 equal portions and mold each into an oval shape. Arrange the 6 slices of cooked eggplant on a large metal platter or roasting pan and place the ovals of stuffing on them. Sprinkle the stuffed eggplants with the remaining bread crumb–cheese mixture and bake under the broiler until golden brown, approximately 3 to 4 minutes. Serve at once.

SERVES 6

CREOLE BOUILLABAISSE

How Jean Galatoire must have longed for the rich, aromatic bouillabaisse of his southern French homeland. How fortuitous that he found in New Orleans many appropriate substitutes for the red rascasse and mussels that enliven the French version of the dish.

Like the French original this Creole version is made with an assortment of fish and shellfish, onions, tomatoes, white wine, garlic, saffron, and herbs, and hearty garlic bread accompanies it to the table. If you would like to use only one species of fish, double the quantity.

4 LARGE TOMATOES

¾ CUP CLARIFIED BUTTER (PAGE 248)

1 CUP FINELY CHOPPED SCALLIONS (GREEN AND WHITE PARTS)

1 LARGE ONION, CHOPPED (ABOUT 1 CUP)

1 TABLESPOON FRESH THYME LEAVES

3 BAY LEAVES

3 TABLESPOONS MINCED GARLIC

1½ CUPS DRY WHITE WINE

1¼ CUPS ALL-PURPOSE FLOUR

1 TABLESPOON HOT PAPRIKA

6 CUPS FISH STOCK (PAGE 117)

3 CUPS OYSTER LIQUOR (MAY SUBSTITUTE ADDITIONAL FISH STOCK OR BOTTLED CLAM JUICE)

3 TEASPOONS SALT

1 TEASPOON CAYENNE PEPPER

2 TABLESPOONS SAFFRON

1 LEMON, CUT INTO ⅛-INCH SLICES

2 DOZEN LARGE (21–25 COUNT) LOUISIANA GULF SHRIMP, PEELED

2 DOZEN LARGE GULF OYSTERS (RESERVE THE LIQUOR)

1 POUND JUMBO LUMP CRABMEAT

1 TEASPOON FRESHLY GROUND BLACK PEPPER

1 POUND REDFISH (OR OTHER FIRM, FLAKY FISH), CUT INTO EIGHT 2-OUNCE PIECES

1 POUND TROUT (OR OTHER FIRM, FLAKY FISH), CUT INTO EIGHT 2-OUNCE PIECES

GARLIC BREAD CUT INTO ROUNDS, FOR GARNISH

Bring 1 quart of water to a boil in a medium saucepan. Blanch the tomatoes in the water about 1 minute, just until the skin breaks. Remove the hot tomatoes from the water and drain. Allow them to cool for 10 minutes, then pull off the skin. Seed and coarsely dice the tomatoes, then set them aside.

In a large stockpot, heat ¼ cup of the clarified butter over high heat. Add the scallions, onions, tomatoes, thyme, and bay leaves and simmer for 10 minutes, stirring occasionally. Add the garlic and white wine and simmer over high heat for an additional 10 minutes, or until most of the wine has cooked away. Whisk ¼ cup of the flour and the paprika into the ingredients and whisk continuously for 5 minutes. Add the fish stock and oyster liquor to the pot and simmer for

30 minutes to allow the flavors to marry and the stock to reduce. Add 2 teaspoons of the salt and the cayenne, saffron, lemon slices, shrimp, and oysters to the stock and simmer for an additional 10 minutes. Remove the stock from the heat and fold in the crabmeat. Remove the bay leaves. Set aside.

Heat the remaining ½ cup of clarified butter in a large sauté pan over high heat. Mix the remaining cup of flour, the remaining teaspoon of salt, and the black pepper in a mixing bowl. Dust the fish pieces in the seasoned flour. Place the fish pieces into the hot pan and sauté for 3 minutes on each side, or until golden. Remove the fish to a platter lined with paper towels and pat dry.

Place 1 piece of each type of fish in the centers of 8 large rimmed soup plates. Ladle the bouillabaisse over the fish and serve immediately with garlic bread rounds.

SERVES 8

Note: Oyster liquor is the water that comes from the oysters when they are shucked. Oysters are sold in this water. If the measurement does not equal 3 cups, add enough cold water to complete the measurement.

Meat, Game, and Poultry Entrées

WHEN ASKED, "Where does the Galatoire's mystique come from?" Chris Ansel, Jr., grandson of Justin Galatoire, replied, "We have worked so hard to keep everything the same. What you get is always the same and you are free to recall memories you have from other times when you were at the restaurant. That it never changes comes as reassuring in a world that is, otherwise, so very uncertain."

This statement holds particularly true of the selections of meat, game, and poultry entrées that Galatoire's has always offered on the everyday menu. Very few of the items have changed since the early twentieth century. The vast majority of Galatoire's meat dishes are simply prepared and adorned with classic French sauces, and it is largely the quality of the raw product that makes the dishes stand out. We use only the very finest cuts available and suggest that you do, too.

The poultry dishes, on the other hand, are a bit more elaborate and often bear names that give no indication of the ingredients. Chicken Financière is one example. There is nothing to indicate the presence of the ham, mushrooms, and veal demi-glace, which have made it a celebrated favorite for most of Galatoire's history. Modern palates delight in all of the unique old-fashioned dishes just waiting to be discovered at Galatoire's, such as Chicken Clemenceau. Few can imagine just how sublime the final outcome is when humble chicken is combined with fried potatoes, canned peas, mushrooms, and a lethal dose of garlic.

As accompaniments to these often substantial entrées we suggest only simple salads, such as the Green Salad with Garlic (page 91), and/or a classic vegetable preparation, such as Broiled Eggplant (page 211) or Julienned Potatoes (page 215).

FILET WITH CARAMELIZED ONIONS AND BLUE CHEESE

The classic pairing of beef and blue cheese is greatly enhanced by the addition of sweetly caramelized onions.

4 TABLESPOONS (½ STICK) SALTED BUTTER

4 YELLOW ONIONS, JULIENNED (ABOUT 4 CUPS)

1 TEASPOON MINCED GARLIC

SALT AND FRESHLY GROUND BLACK PEPPER TO TASTE

SIX 10-OUNCE CENTER-CUT BEEF FILETS

¼ CUP OLIVE OIL

6 TABLESPOONS CRUMBLED BLUE CHEESE

Preheat an outdoor gas or charcoal grill.

Melt the butter in a large nonstick sauté pan over high heat. Add the onions and sauté for 6 to 8 minutes, until the onions start to caramelize. Deglaze the pan with ¼ cup water to moisten the onions and lift any sugars that are on the bottom of the pan. Reduce for 2 to 3 minutes, until most of the liquid has evaporated. Add the garlic, season with salt and pepper, toss, and set aside.

Preheat the broiler in the oven.

Brush the filets with the olive oil and season with salt and pepper. Place the filets on the preheated grill and cook for 6 to 8 minutes on each side, until the meat is medium rare. Remove from the grill to an ovenproof pan.

Evenly mound the caramelized onions atop the filets and place 1 tablespoon of crumbled blue cheese atop each mound. Heat the steaks under the preheated broiler for 2 minutes, or until the cheese is bubbling and melted. Serve at once.

SERVES 6

FILET FOIE GRAS WITH SHIITAKE MUSHROOM AND TRUFFLE OIL DEMI-GLACE

The decadent combination of filet foie gras and truffle oil makes this dish worthy of a king. Truffles have been prized by gourmands for centuries and were credited by the ancient Greeks and Romans with both therapeutic and aphrodisiac powers. Though only a scant amount of truffle oil is added to the sauce just before serving, its pungent sensuality is immediately discernible.

---

2 TABLESPOONS SALTED BUTTER

4 OUNCES SHIITAKE MUSHROOM CAPS (ABOUT 2 CUPS), SLICED

1 TEASPOON MINCED GARLIC

SALT AND FRESHLY GROUND BLACK PEPPER TO TASTE

3 CUPS VEAL DEMI-GLACE (PAGE 267)

SIX 10-OUNCE CENTER-CUT BEEF FILETS

1/4 CUP OLIVE OIL

SIX 3-OUNCE PORTIONS OF FOIE GRAS, ABOUT 3/4 INCH THICK

1/2 TEASPOON TRUFFLE OIL

Preheat an outdoor gas or charcoal grill.

Melt the butter in a medium sauté pan over medium-high heat. Add the mushrooms and sauté for 2 minutes, or until tender. Add the garlic, toss briefly, and season with salt and pepper. Add the demi-glace and reduce the heat to medium-low while you prepare the filets and foie gras. Upon completion the sauce should be thick and syrupy enough to coat the back of a spoon.

Brush the filets with olive oil and season with salt and pepper. Place on the preheated grill. Cook for 6 to 8 minutes on each side depending on the thickness of the cut and the doneness desired. Medium rare is recommended.

About 5 minutes before the filet is finished cooking on the grill, preheat a large sauté pan over high heat for the foie gras. Remove the filet from the grill to an oven to keep it warm while the foie gras is prepared.

Place the foie gras into the extremely hot pan to sear. Cook for 30 to 45 seconds on each side until a golden crust forms. Immediately remove from the pan to a plate.

Center the filets on each of 6 dinner plates. Place a piece of seared foie gras atop each filet. Stir the truffle oil into the warm mushroom demi-glace and nap the sauce over the filet and foie gras. Serve immediately.

SERVES 6

SIRLOIN MARCHAND DE VIN

The dense though versatile Marchand de Vin sauce works particularly well with sirloin steak (New York strip).

3 TABLESPOONS SALTED BUTTER

4 OUNCES BUTTON MUSHROOMS (ABOUT 1½ CUPS), SLICED

SALT AND FRESHLY GROUND BLACK PEPPER TO TASTE

¼ CUP FINELY DICED HAM (ABOUT 1 OUNCE)

¼ CUP THINLY SLICED SCALLIONS (GREEN AND WHITE PARTS)

1 TABLESPOON ALL-PURPOSE FLOUR

1 CUP RED WINE

3 CUPS VEAL DEMI-GLACE (PAGE 267)

SIX 14-OUNCE SIRLOIN STEAKS (NEW YORK STRIPS), CUT 1½ TO 2 INCHES THICK

Preheat an outdoor gas or charcoal grill.

In a medium sauté pan over high heat, melt the butter. Add the mushrooms and sauté for 3 minutes, or until tender. Season with salt and pepper. Add the ham, scallions, and flour to the pan and sauté for an additional 3 minutes, or until the ingredients start to brown in the pan. Deglaze the pan with the red wine and simmer for 6 to 8 minutes, until the volume of the liquid is reduced by half. Add the demi-glace and reduce the heat to medium. Allow the sauce to simmer while you grill the steaks. Upon completion the sauce should be thick enough to coat the back of a spoon.

Season the steaks liberally with salt and pepper. Place them on the grill and cook for 6 to 8 minutes on each side depending on the thickness of the steaks, until they are the desired doneness. Medium rare is recommended. Remove the steaks from the grill.

Nap the sauce across the centers of the steaks and serve immediately.

SERVES 6

VEAL LIVER WITH BACON AND ONIONS

This preparation for veal liver is popular in the Lyonnais region of France and was, undoubtedly, familiar to Jean Galatoire and his family. The ingredients are inexpensive and available anywhere in the world. The smokiness of the bacon and the sweet onion are universally satisfying complements to the silky, rich veal liver.

8 THICK SLICES OF HICKORY-SMOKED BACON

4 TABLESPOONS (½ STICK) SALTED BUTTER

4 CUPS JULIENNED ONIONS (ABOUT 4 MEDIUM ONIONS)

1 TEASPOON MINCED GARLIC

SALT AND FRESHLY GROUND BLACK PEPPER TO TASTE

1 CUP CLARIFIED BUTTER (PAGE 248)

EIGHT 4-OUNCE SLICES OF VEAL LIVER

2 CUPS ALL-PURPOSE FLOUR

¼ CUP CHOPPED CURLY PARSLEY, FOR GARNISH

Fry the bacon in a large sauté pan until crisp. Remove to a plate lined with paper towels while preparing the rest of the dish.

Melt the salted butter in a large nonstick sauté pan over high heat. Add the onions and sauté for 8 to 10 minutes, until they start to caramelize. Deglaze the pan with ¼ cup water to moisten the onions and lift any sugars that are on the bottom of the pan. Add the garlic to the pan, season with salt and pepper, toss, and remove the pan from the heat. Set the onions aside while preparing the liver.

To a separate large sauté pan over high heat, add ½ cup of the clarified butter. Season the veal liver with salt and pepper, then dust the slices with flour, shaking off any excess. Add half of the veal liver slices to the pan. Adjust the heat to medium and cook for 2 to 3 minutes, until a golden brown crust forms. Turn the slices and cook for another 2 to 3 minutes, adding more clarified butter if necessary. Carefully lift the slices from the pan and drain on paper towels.

Add the remaining ½ cup clarified butter to the pan and repeat the cooking process for the remaining slices of veal liver, raising the heat back to high at the start of the cooking process if the pan has cooled.

Place 2 pieces of liver on each plate. Equally distribute the caramelized onions atop the liver. Garnish the dish by placing the slices of bacon in an "X" atop the onions. Sprinkle with chopped parsley.

SERVES 4

VEAL RIB CHOPS WITH ROASTED SHALLOTS AND BACON LARDON DEMI-GLACE

Don't be daunted by the list of ingredients in this dish. The most complex component is the demi-glace, which can be made well in advance and will keep, refrigerated, in a sealed jar for two weeks. If frozen, it will keep for six months. Cheaters can use high-quality store-bought demi-glace for this dish, making it easy to prepare on cold winter days when it will be most appreciated.

Creamy mashed potatoes would be an ideal accompaniment.

---

6 LARGE SHALLOTS, PEELED

1 CUP OLIVE OIL

LEAVES FROM 3 SPRIGS OF FRESH THYME

KOSHER SALT AND FRESHLY GROUND BLACK PEPPER
    TO TASTE

1 POUND SMOKED SLAB BACON

2 CUPS VEAL DEMI-GLACE (PAGE 267)

6 VEAL RIB CHOPS (12 TO 14 OUNCES EACH)

Preheat the oven to 200°F. Place the shallots and olive oil in a small glass baking dish. Add the thyme and season with salt and pepper. Toss the shallots to coat them with the oil, then bake for 2 hours, or until the shallots are tender and golden.

Cut the bacon into ¼-inch cubes (lardons) and spread them on a baking sheet. Place in the oven with the shallots and bake for approximately 1 hour, until the fat is rendered. Drain the lardons on paper towels and reserve the rendered fat for another use.

Remove the shallots from the baking dish with a slotted spoon, reserving the olive oil. Heat the demi-glace in a small saucepan over low heat for 5 to 6 minutes, until simmering. Add the shallots and lardons, stirring gently to maintain the shape of the shallots. Keep the sauce warm over very low heat while you grill the veal chops.

Heat a grill until it is red hot. Season the veal chops with salt and pepper and then brush them with the reserved shallot-and-thyme-infused olive oil. When the grill is ready brush it also with the infused oil. Grill the chops to medium rare (or personal preference), 4 to 5 minutes on each side.

Center the grilled chops on warmed plates. Using a slotted spoon, remove the shallots from the demi-glace and arrange them over the chops. Ladle ¼ cup of the sauce with lardons over each chop. Serve immediately.

SERVES 6

DOUBLE-CUT PORK CHOPS WITH CREOLE MUSTARD AND SOUTHERN COMFORT GLAZE

In 1874, in the comfort of his bar near Bourbon Street, M. W. Heron developed the potent, sweet liqueur that would evolve into Southern Comfort. Soon after, he left New Orleans for Memphis, and took his popular tonic with him, making it unlikely that Galatoire's founder, Jean Galatoire, would have been exposed to Heron's still-obscure brew upon his arrival to the city.

One hundred years later Jean Galatoire's cuisine and Mr. Heron's exotic libation are married to delicious effect in a glaze that is the perfect foil for hefty double-cut pork chops.

¼ CUP SOUTHERN COMFORT LIQUEUR

¼ CUP CREOLE MUSTARD OR ANY COARSE, GRAINY
    BROWN MUSTARD

¼ CUP HONEY

2 CUPS VEAL DEMI-GLACE (PAGE 267)

6 DOUBLE-CUT PORK CHOPS

SALT AND FRESHLY GROUND BLACK PEPPER TO TASTE

Preheat an outdoor gas or charcoal grill.

Heat the Southern Comfort in a medium sauté pan over high heat. Once the liqueur is hot, tilt the pan. The liquor will flow to the side of the pan and the cooking flame will ignite it. If you are cooking with an electric stove, carefully ignite the liquor with a long kitchen match. Allow the flame to burn for a moment to cook off some of the alcohol. Whisk in the Creole mustard and the honey. Add the demi-glace and reduce the heat to low. While the pork chops are being grilled, allow the sauce to simmer and reduce until it is syrupy. The sauce should be thick enough to coat the back of a spoon.

Season the pork chops liberally with salt and pepper and place them on the grill. Cook the chops for 8 to 10 minutes on each side depending on the thickness. Cook to an internal temperature from 150°F to 165°F for medium, the recommended doneness.

Sauce the chops with the Southern Comfort glaze and serve at once.

SERVES 6

VENISON FILET WITH JUNIPER BERRY DEMI-GLACE AND ROASTED SWEET POTATOES

The assertive flavor of the juniper berries successfully stands up to the equally assertive venison, while the soft, sweet flavor and texture of the potatoes makes for an unexpected though welcome pairing. This is a wholly satisfying dish that should be particularly well received when it is cold outdoors.

Please note: While they are attractive, the juniper berries are left in the sauce solely as a garnish and should not be eaten. They are safe to ingest but their flavor is undesirably astringent when they are consumed whole. They should be soaked overnight in the brandy. Be sure to allow enough preparation time.

¼ CUP BRANDY

6 TABLESPOONS DRIED JUNIPER BERRIES

1 TEASPOON SALT, PLUS ADDITIONAL TO TASTE

½ TEASPOON CAYENNE PEPPER

1 TEASPOON LIGHT BROWN SUGAR

½ TEASPOON CINNAMON

3 LARGE SWEET POTATOES, PEELED AND CUT INTO
    EIGHTHS

½ CUP OLIVE OIL

2 TABLESPOONS HONEY

3 CUPS VEAL DEMI-GLACE (PAGE 267)

6 VENISON FILETS, EACH ABOUT 8 OUNCES

FRESHLY GROUND BLACK PEPPER TO TASTE

Combine the brandy and juniper berries and allow the berries to soak overnight.

Preheat the oven to 350°F.

Combine the salt, cayenne pepper, brown sugar, and cinnamon in a small bowl. Place the sweet potatoes and ¼ cup of the olive oil in a large roasting pan and toss to coat the potatoes. Add the spice mixture and toss again. Spread the potatoes in a single layer across the bottom of the roasting pan and bake for 45 minutes to an hour, until the potatoes are tender. Prepare the venison while the sweet potatoes are in the oven.

Preheat an outdoor gas or charcoal grill.

Add the mixture of brandy and juniper berries to a medium saucepan over high heat. Once the liquor is hot, tilt the pan. The liquor will flow to the side of the pan and the cooking flame will ignite it. If you are cooking with an electric stove, carefully ignite the liquor with a long kitchen match. Allow the flame to burn for a moment to cook off some of the alcohol. Add the honey and the veal demi-glace to the pan and reduce the heat to low. Allow the sauce to simmer over low heat while you grill the venison. Upon completion the sauce should be thick enough to coat the back of a spoon.

Season the venison filets with salt and black pepper and brush them with the remaining ¼ cup olive oil before placing them on the grill. Cook over high heat for 5 minutes on each side to obtain a rosy medium, the recommended doneness.

Place the grilled venison filets in the centers of each of 6 dinner plates. Nap the juniper demi-glace atop the filets and arrange the roasted sweet potatoes around them. Serve at once.

SERVES 6

LAMB CHOPS WITH CURRANT AND MOREL DEMI-GLACE

The sweetness of the currant jelly cuts cleanly through the demi-glace. When entertaining, you can prepare the morel demi-glace hours in advance. Simply reheat the sauce while the lamb is grilling and add the currant jelly just before serving.

1 OUNCE DRIED MOREL MUSHROOMS

3 CUPS VEAL DEMI-GLACE (PAGE 267)

12 DOUBLE-CUT DOMESTIC LAMB CHOPS (6 TO 8 OUNCES
    EACH), FRENCHED

SALT AND FRESHLY GROUND BLACK PEPPER TO TASTE

¼ CUP PREMIUM-QUALITY CURRANT JELLY

Steep the mushrooms in enough hot water to cover for 2 to 3 minutes, or until soft. Drain the mushrooms, and then slice them into rings.

Preheat an outdoor gas or charcoal grill.

Heat the demi-glace in a medium saucepan over high heat. Once it begins to simmer, add the mushrooms and reduce the heat to medium. Allow the sauce to simmer lightly while you cook the lamb chops. The sauce should reduce to a syrupy consistency that coats the back of a spoon.

Season the chops liberally with the salt and pepper. Place the chops on the preheated grill and cook to the desired doneness. Medium rare is recommended and will take approximately 5 to 6 minutes on each side. Be cautious of flare-ups due to the high fat content of lamb. If this occurs, simply shift the position of the chops on the grill. Remove the chops from the grill.

Stir the currant jelly into the simmering demi-glace. Stir to incorporate and heat for 2 minutes, or until blended.

Center 2 chops on each of 6 dinner plates and gently top the chops with the currant and morel demi-glace. Serve at once.

SERVES 6

CHICKEN BONNE FEMME

In this case the "good woman" (bonne femme) is indulging in simple, hearty, delicious food. This classic French bistro dish is a meal in itself and would need only a simple green salad as an accompaniment, if anything at all.

½ POUND SLICED BACON	2 LARGE ONIONS, JULIENNED (ABOUT 4 CUPS)
1 FRYER CHICKEN, CUT INTO 8 PIECES	1 TABLESPOON MINCED GARLIC
SALT AND FRESHLY GROUND BLACK PEPPER TO TASTE	2 LARGE IDAHO POTATOES, PEELED AND CUT INTO
VEGETABLE OIL, FOR FRYING	⅛-INCH-THICK SLICES
4 TABLESPOONS (½ STICK) SALTED BUTTER	¼ CUP CHOPPED CURLY PARSLEY, FOR GARNISH

Preheat the oven to 400°F.

Fry the bacon in a large sauté pan until crisp. Remove to a plate lined with paper towels while preparing the rest of the dish.

Rinse the chicken pieces and dry them thoroughly. Season the chicken generously with salt and pepper and bake on a rimmed baking sheet for approximately 30 minutes until golden brown, turning the pieces after 15 minutes.

While the chicken is baking, begin preparing the bonne femme garnish.

In a large, heavy-bottomed pot suitable for frying, heat the vegetable oil to 350°F.

In a separate large nonstick sauté pan over high heat, melt the butter. Add the onions and sauté for 8 to 10 minutes, until they start to become caramelized. Deglaze the pan with ½ cup of water to moisten the onions and lift any sugars that are on the bottom of the pan. Crumble the bacon into the onions and add the garlic to the hot pan. Toss to combine the ingredients, remove from the heat, and set aside.

Deep-fry the potatoes in the vegetable oil until they are golden brown. Remove them with a slotted spoon to drain on paper towels, and season with salt and pepper.

Toss the potatoes with the bacon and onions and set aside. This is the bonne femme garnish.

When the chicken is golden brown, divide the bonne femme atop the chicken pieces and bake together for an additional 3 minutes.

Divide the chicken bonne femme among 4 dinner plates. Finish the dish by sprinkling each portion with chopped parsley. Serve immediately.

SERVES 4

CHICKEN CLEMENCEAU

French statesman Georges Clemenceau (1841–1929) is credited with bringing France from the brink of defeat to victory in World War One. In part he did so by convincing the Allies to unify their efforts through the leadership of a supreme commander, previously unheard of among nations of the day. Equally unheard of was the amalgamation of chicken, fried potatoes, garlic, mushrooms, and canned peas into a single dish, as was achieved here at Galatoire's in the 1920s to delicious effect. The dish is named for Monsieur Clemenceau.

---

1 FRYER CHICKEN, CUT INTO 8 PIECES

SALT AND FRESHLY GROUND WHITE PEPPER TO TASTE

1 GALLON VEGETABLE OIL

2 BAKING POTATOES

¼ CUP CLARIFIED BUTTER (PAGE 248)

1 POUND LARGE BUTTON MUSHROOMS, CLEANED AND
    SLICED

3 TABLESPOONS MINCED GARLIC

ONE 15-OUNCE CAN PETIT POIS PEAS, DRAINED

CHOPPED CURLY PARSLEY, FOR GARNISH

Preheat the oven to 400°F. Rinse the chicken and dry thoroughly. Season it generously with salt and pepper and bake on a rimmed baking sheet for approximately 30 minutes, until golden brown, turning the pieces after 15 minutes.

While the chicken is baking, heat the oil in a large heavy-bottomed pot to 350°F. Peel the potatoes and dice them into ¾-inch cubes. When the oil is hot, add the potatoes, about 1 cup at a time. The moisture content in the potatoes will make the oil boil up, so use a long-handled spoon when adding. Fry the potatoes in batches, about 7 to 9 minutes each batch, until golden brown, moving the cubes around with the spoon to ensure that all sides brown evenly. Remove the potatoes from the oil with a slotted spoon and drain on paper towels.

Heat the butter in a large sauté pan over high heat, then add the mushrooms. Cook the mushrooms for about 5 minutes, until tender. Add the garlic and the fried potatoes. Season with salt and white pepper and sauté briefly to heat through. Add the chicken pieces and sauté for 3 to 5 minutes, until the flavors marry. Gently fold in the petit pois and cook until just heated through.

Divide the chicken Clemenceau among 4 dinner plates using a slotted spoon to drain any excess butter. Finish the dish by sprinkling each portion with chopped parsley. Serve immediately.

SERVES 6

CHICKEN CREOLE

This simple, elegant, lovely dish is a standard on the New Orleans Sunday dinner table.

4 RIPE TOMATOES

1 FRYER CHICKEN, CUT INTO 8 PIECES

2 TEASPOONS SALT, PLUS ADDITIONAL TO TASTE

FRESHLY GROUND BLACK PEPPER TO TASTE

2 TABLESPOONS SALTED BUTTER

1 CELERY STALK, DICED (ABOUT ½ CUP)

1 SMALL GREEN BELL PEPPER, DICED (ABOUT 1 CUP)

2 ONIONS, DICED (ABOUT 1½ CUPS)

¼ CUP TOMATO PASTE

1 BAY LEAF

1 TEASPOON CAYENNE PEPPER

1 TEASPOON HOT PAPRIKA

3 CUPS CHICKEN STOCK

3 CUPS STEAMED WHITE RICE

¼ CUP CHOPPED CURLY PARSLEY, FOR GARNISH

Preheat the oven to 400°F. Bring 1 quart of water to a boil in a medium saucepan.

Blanch the tomatoes in the water about 1 minute, just until the skin breaks. Remove the hot tomatoes from the water and drain. Allow them to cool for 10 minutes, then pull off the skin and discard it. Seed and coarsely dice the tomatoes, then set them aside.

Rinse the chicken pieces and dry them thoroughly. Season the chicken generously with salt and black pepper and bake on a rimmed baking sheet for approximately 30 minutes, until golden brown, turning the pieces after 15 minutes.

While the chicken is baking, begin making the Creole sauce. Melt the butter in a large stockpot over high heat. Add the celery, bell peppers, onions, and tomatoes and sauté for 7 to 10 minutes, until the tomatoes are nearly dissolved and the vegetables begin to caramelize. Reduce the heat to medium and add the tomato paste, bay leaf, 2 teaspoons of salt, the cayenne pepper, and paprika. Allow the mixture to simmer for an additional 3 to 4 minutes. Add the chicken stock, raise the heat to medium-high, and bring it to a boil. Reduce the heat to medium and cook for 20 minutes, or until the sauce is slightly thickened.

Remove the chicken from the oven and add the pieces to the pot of Creole sauce. Simmer the chicken and sauce together for 5 minutes.

Serve the chicken Creole with the steamed white rice and garnish with the parsley.

SERVES 4

CHICKEN FINANCIÈRE

Since its opening in 1905 Galatoire's has been located at 209 Bourbon Street, just across Canal Street from New Orleans's busy financial district. The Parisian bistros where this dish originated enjoyed a similar proximity to France's bustling center of commerce. It is only fitting that Jean Galatoire would choose to include this aptly named, indisputably rich dish (which is created from rather humble ingredients) on his restaurant's menu from the very beginning. The same version is still served today.

1 FRYER CHICKEN, CUT INTO 8 PIECES

SALT AND FRESHLY GROUND BLACK PEPPER TO TASTE

3 TABLESPOONS SALTED BUTTER

4 OUNCES SLICED BUTTON MUSHROOMS (ABOUT 1½ CUPS)

¼ CUP FINELY DICED HAM (ABOUT 1 OUNCE)

¼ CUP SCALLIONS, THINLY SLICED (GREEN AND WHITE PARTS)

1 CHICKEN LIVER, CHOPPED

6 RIPE GREEN OLIVES, PITTED AND SLICED LENGTHWISE

1 TABLESPOON ALL-PURPOSE FLOUR

1 CUP RED WINE

3 CUPS VEAL DEMI-GLACE (PAGE 267)

¼ CUP CHOPPED CURLY PARSLEY, FOR GARNISH

Preheat the oven to 400°F.

Rinse the chicken and dry thoroughly. Season the chicken generously with salt and pepper and bake on a rimmed baking sheet for approximately 30 minutes, until golden brown, turning the pieces after 15 minutes.

In a medium sauté pan over high heat, melt the butter. Add the mushrooms and sauté for 3 minutes, or until tender. Season the mushrooms with salt and pepper and add the ham, scallions, liver, olives, and flour and sauté for an additional 3 minutes, or until the ingredients start to brown in the pan. Deglaze the pan with the wine and simmer for 6 to 8 minutes, until the liquid is reduced by half. Add the demi-glace, bring the mixture to a boil, and reduce the heat to medium. Allow the sauce to cook at a low rolling boil for 20 minutes, or until it has a thick, rich consistency that coats the back of a spoon.

Remove the chicken from the oven and place it in the financière sauce. Simmer for 4 to 5 minutes. Serve immediately.

SERVES 4

CHICKEN ROCHAMBEAU

Another historic New Orleans restaurant, Antoine's, is credited with the creation of this New Orleans classic. Antoine's founder, Antoine Alciatore, named the dish for Jean-Baptiste Donatien de Vimeur, the Comte de Rochambeau, one of the most important foreign military commanders to fight for the United States during the American Revolution. Born into great wealth and opulence at Vendôme, Rochambeau would no doubt have appreciated the sinfully rich, flavorful dish that is named in his honor.

4 BONELESS, SKINLESS 5-OUNCE SPLIT CHICKEN
   BREASTS

4 HAM SLICES, EACH ¼ INCH THICK AND THE SHAPE OF
   THE CHICKEN BREAST

3 TABLESPOONS SALTED BUTTER

4 SLICES OF WHITE BREAD

3 CUPS MARCHAND DE VIN SAUCE (PAGE 262), WARMED

2 CUPS BÉARNAISE SAUCE (PAGE 250)

In a medium sauté pan, bring 1 quart of water to a low boil over high heat. Add the chicken and ham and poach for 6 minutes, or until the chicken is cooked through.

Prepare the toast points while the chicken and ham are poaching: In a large sauté pan over low heat, melt the butter. Add the slices of bread. Cook for 1 to 2 minutes on each side until golden. Remove the bread from the pan; slice off and discard the crusts. Cut the toast in half diagonally. You will have 8 toast points.

Place a ham slice on each plate. Equally distribute warm marchand de vin sauce atop the slices. Place a split chicken breast atop the ham slice and marchand de vin. Nap warm béarnaise sauce on the chicken. Garnish each plate with 2 toast points. Serve immediately.

SERVES 4

The Galatoire family is proud to play a part in so many New Orleanians' significant memories and traditions. Their commitment to preserving others' family traditions stems from their own rich family heritage. Simone Galatoire Nugent, daughter of René and Rosemary Galatoire, shared her memories of some of her family's holiday traditions, which continue to this day.

"As I grew up we held all family dinners at my parents' home. Both of my parents loved to have a house full of people and both of them loved to cook. The door was always open to everyone— and they came.

"Thanksgiving and Christmas were always my mother's favorite holidays, times when she could really shine in the kitchen and dress up the house. Thanksgiving dinner was always very lavish and traditional with plenty of turkey, mashed potatoes, green peas, meat dressing, pecan and mincemeat pies—and, always, my mother's oyster patties. Even today, Thanksgiving is not complete without them.

"I remember going to the home of my aunt and uncle John and Clarisse Gooch on Christmas Eve when I was a *very* young child, but at some point my parents decided to start their own tradition. For about forty years my mother and father hosted a big Christmas Eve party. The table was laden with boiled shrimp, fresh crabmeat, raw oysters, lobster, salmon, and homemade sweets. We baked ham and turkey and made party sandwiches. Our family friend Tula Cory always brought wonderful homemade muffulettas [a hearty, native New Orleans sandwich made with salami, ham, provolone, and olive salad].

"There were oyster patties there, too.

"Santa Claus even came to pass out gifts to all the children!

"This tradition continued until my oldest child, Renée, was about five and it became very difficult to bring all of Santa's gifts to New Orleans. So we began our own Christmas Eve tradition in Baton Rouge and my mother, sister, aunt, and extended family help us celebrate. But the whole family still gathers together prior to Christmas for a special family celebration . . . and we still eat oyster patties."

CHICKEN SAINT-PIERRE

This is New Orleans home-style comfort food: a simple, flavorful, satisfying dish that is easy to prepare with ingredients most of us already have on hand. Serve this with plenty of warm French bread for mopping up the delicious sauce.

2 LARGE RIPE TOMATOES

1 FRYER CHICKEN, CUT INTO 8 PIECES

1 TEASPOON SALT, PLUS ADDITIONAL TO TASTE

FRESHLY GROUND BLACK PEPPER TO TASTE

2 TABLESPOONS SALTED BUTTER

8 OUNCES BUTTON MUSHROOMS, SLICED (ABOUT 2 CUPS)

¼ CUP FINELY SLICED SCALLIONS (WHITE AND GREEN PARTS)

2 TABLESPOONS MINCED GARLIC

1 TEASPOON CAYENNE PEPPER

½ CUP WHITE WINE

2 CUPS CHICKEN STOCK

Preheat the oven to 400°F.

Bring 1 quart of water to a boil in a medium saucepan. Blanch the tomatoes in the water about 1 minute, just until the skin breaks. Remove the hot tomatoes from the water and drain. Allow to cool for 10 minutes, then pull off the skin and discard it. Seed and coarsely dice the tomatoes, then set them aside.

Rinse the chicken pieces, dry thoroughly, and season generously with salt and black pepper. Place the pieces in a large baking dish and bake for approximately 30 minutes, until the skin is golden brown, turning the pieces after 15 minutes.

While the chicken is baking, begin preparing the Saint-Pierre sauce: In a large sauté pan over high heat, melt the butter. Add the mushrooms and sauté for 2 minutes, or until tender. Add the scallions and tomatoes and sauté for 2 to 3 minutes, until the tomatoes begin to stick to the pan. Add the garlic, 1 teaspoon salt, and the cayenne pepper and toss briefly. Deglaze the pan with the wine. Sauté for 2 minutes to cook some of the wine off, and add the chicken stock. Simmer over high heat for 4 to 5 minutes, allowing the mixture to reduce slightly and the flavors to combine.

Remove the chicken from the oven and add it to the Saint-Pierre sauce. Simmer the chicken in the sauce for 3 to 4 additional minutes. Serve at once.

SERVES 4

Galatoire's Fried Chicken

Fried chicken is synonymous with the South and everyone's family recipe is "the best." While some involve elaborate marinades and spices and unusual crushed ingredients in the batter, this one is about as simple as it gets.

This recipe yields a thick, crunchy, satisfying coating that seals moisture into the chicken and retains the juices until you take that first savored bite. The keys to achieving perfect results are fully coating the chicken in the egg wash and flour and carefully monitoring the oil temperature during cooking.

Oil, for frying

3 large eggs

3 cups whole milk

3 cups all-purpose flour

One 2½- to 3-pound frying chicken, cut into 8 pieces

Salt and freshly ground black pepper to taste

Using a candy thermometer to maintain the temperature, heat the oil to 350°F in a large, heavy-bottomed pot suitable for frying.

In a large mixing bowl, combine the eggs and milk to form an egg wash. Place the flour in a separate large mixing bowl. Season the chicken with salt and pepper and dredge it in the flour. Remove the chicken from the flour and shake off the excess. Submerge the chicken in egg wash. Remove the chicken from the egg wash and dredge it in the flour a second time. Shake off the excess flour and place the chicken into the hot oil. Monitor the temperature of the oil with the thermometer while cooking to make sure the temperature doesn't drop too low when you add the chicken or spike too high once it has recovered. Cook for 12 to 15 minutes, until the chicken begins to float in the oil. The smaller pieces might cook faster than the larger ones. With a slotted spoon or tongs, remove the chicken from the oil to a platter lined with paper towels. Allow the chicken to cool until it can be touched, about 5 minutes.

Serves 4

Vegetables and Side Dishes

THE MOST POPULAR VEGETABLE DISHES at Galatoire's are simple steamed asparagus or broccoli, served either buttered or with a side of hollandaise sauce. Broiled Eggplant, Hash Brown Potatoes, and Creamed Spinach are also straightforward choices for the busy home cook and they pair well with just about anything.

With our more elaborate vegetable preparations, such as Lyonnaise Potatoes, Potatoes au Gratin, or Brabant Potatoes, the very French heritage of Galatoire's is immediately discernible.

As with other dishes, the success of our vegetable executions depends upon the quality of the raw ingredients.

In the days before produce was delivered to the restaurant, Jean Galatoire and a helper from the restaurant would visit New Orleans's French Market every morning at sunrise to hand-select fresh produce and carry it back to

Galatoire's. Delivery services have added convenience to the process, but the

emphasis on freshness remains.

B R A B A N T   P O T A T O E S

These are delicious fried potato cubes tossed with butter and pungent garlic. Brabant *refers to the shape.*

OIL, FOR FRYING

8 IDAHO POTATOES

½ CUP CLARIFIED BUTTER (PAGE 248), WARMED

2 TABLESPOONS MINCED GARLIC

3 TABLESPOONS CHOPPED CURLY PARSLEY

SALT AND FRESHLY GROUND BLACK PEPPER TO TASTE

Place the oil in a heavy-bottomed pot suited for frying and heat to 350° F. Check the temperature with a candy thermometer.

Peel the potatoes and cut them into ¾-inch cubes while waiting for the oil to get hot.

Add the potatoes to the oil and fry for 8 to 10 minutes, until golden brown and tender. Use a slotted spoon to remove the potatoes from the oil to a platter lined with paper towels to drain briefly.

Place the fried potatoes in a large mixing bowl and add the warm butter, garlic, and parsley, and season with salt and pepper. Toss until the potatoes are evenly coated. Serve at once.

SERVES 6

BROCCOLI OR CAULIFLOWER AU GRATIN

To achieve the most desirable result—a crisp, golden crust—you'll want to create maximum surface exposure in the baking dish.

---

1 LARGE CROWN OF BROCCOLI, STEAMED, OR 1 LARGE
    HEAD OF CAULIFLOWER, STEAMED, OR A MIXTURE OF
    BOTH
2 CUPS BÉCHAMEL SAUCE (PAGE 251)
2 CUPS SHREDDED SHARP CHEDDAR CHEESE

SALT AND FRESHLY GROUND WHITE PEPPER TO TASTE
2 LARGE EGG YOLKS, LIGHTLY BEATEN
1 CUP SEASONED DRIED BREAD CRUMBS
¼ CUP PARMESAN CHEESE
¼ CUP CLARIFIED BUTTER (PAGE 248)

Preheat a broiler on low.

Coarsely chop the broccoli or cauliflower. Add the broccoli or cauliflower to a large sauté pan over medium heat. Add the béchamel sauce and Cheddar cheese and simmer until all of the cheese is melted. Stir until the ingredients are incorporated and season with salt and pepper. Fold in the egg yolks and remove from the heat.

Transfer the mixture to a 13 × 9 × 2-inch ovenproof dish. Smooth out the top to create an even layer. Mix the bread crumbs and Parmesan cheese together in a small bowl and sprinkle over the contents of the baking dish. Drizzle the clarified butter over the bread crumbs.

Broil for 2 to 3 minutes, until a golden brown crust is formed. Serve immediately.

SERVES 6

BROILED EGGPLANT

Do not slice the eggplant until the very last minute before you pass it under the broiler, or it will develop an undesirable brown hue.

2 LARGE PURPLE EGGPLANTS

½ CUP CLARIFIED BUTTER (PAGE 248)

SALT AND FRESHLY GROUND BLACK PEPPER TO TASTE

2 TABLESPOONS CHOPPED CURLY PARSLEY, FOR GARNISH

Preheat a broiler on low.

Wash and dry the eggplants and slice them into ½-inch rounds. Discard the ends and lay the remaining pieces flat on a jelly-roll pan or cookie sheet. Brush both sides of the eggplant rounds with the clarified butter and season with salt and pepper. Broil the eggplants for 5 minutes, or until they are fork-tender and golden brown.

With a spatula, remove the eggplants from the pan to a serving platter. Drizzle some of the remaining butter atop the eggplants and garnish with chopped parsley. Serve at once.

SERVES 6

GALATOIRE'S CREAMED SPINACH

Creamed Spinach may very well be the most popular vegetable side dish served at Galatoire's. The flavor of the dish is rather mild, making it an appropriate accompaniment for meat, poultry, game, and seafood. Creamed Spinach serves as the base for several dishes at Galatoire's, including Eggs Sardou and Crabmeat Sardou.

When selecting spinach, look for leaves that are crisp and dark green with a clean fragrance.

---

2 POUNDS FRESH SPINACH

1 TABLESPOON UNSALTED BUTTER

½ CUP FINELY CHOPPED ONION

1 CUP BÉCHAMEL SAUCE (PAGE 251)

¼ CUP HEAVY WHIPPING CREAM

SALT AND FRESHLY GROUND WHITE PEPPER TO TASTE

Bring 1 quart of water to a boil in a large saucepan. Cut the stems from the spinach, and wash the leaves in cold water to remove any sand. Add the spinach to the boiling water. Reduce the heat to medium-high and simmer for 3 to 4 minutes, covered, until the spinach is tender. Drain the spinach in a mesh strainer, pressing out the liquid with a spoon. Finely chop the cooked spinach and set aside 3 cups. Any remaining spinach can be frozen for future use.

Melt the butter in a large sauté pan over medium heat. Add the onions and cook for 3 minutes, until the onions are tender. Add the reserved spinach to the pan, then stir in the béchamel and cream. Reduce the heat to low and simmer for 3 minutes, stirring, until the ingredients are thoroughly incorporated and the spinach is heated through. Season with salt and white pepper.

MAKES ABOUT 4 CUPS

JULIENNED POTATOES

These ultrathin, crunchy potatoes are incredibly addictive and work well as an accompaniment to just about everything.

VEGETABLE OIL, FOR FRYING

8 IDAHO POTATOES

SALT AND FRESHLY GROUND BLACK PEPPER TO TASTE

CHOPPED CURLY PARSLEY, FOR GARNISH

Add the oil to a heavy pot suitable for frying and heat the oil to 350°F, using a candy thermometer to check the temperature.

Peel the potatoes and cut them into ¼-inch julienned strips while waiting for the oil to heat.

Fry the potatoes for 4 to 5 minutes, until they are golden brown and tender and float to the top of the oil. Using a slotted spoon, remove the potatoes from the oil to a platter lined with paper towels. Sprinkle with salt and pepper. Garnish with parsley and serve hot.

SERVES 6

HASH BROWN POTATOES

Hash browns are an immensely popular side dish at Galatoire's. They are as appropriate with steak as they are with our many egg dishes.

½ CUP CLARIFIED BUTTER (PAGE 248)

4 IDAHO POTATOES, PEELED, BOILED, AND CUT INTO
  ¼-INCH DICE

SALT AND FRESHLY GROUND WHITE PEPPER TO TASTE

Heat ¼ cup of the clarified butter in a medium sauté pan over high heat. When the butter is hot, add half of the potatoes and use a spatula to press them into the pan to form what resembles a dense cake. Season the potatoes with salt and pepper. Continue to sauté the potato cake for 5 to 8 minutes, until it is a golden brown color. Use the spatula to gently flip the potato cake and brown the other side. Slide the potato cake onto a serving platter and keep warm while you repeat the process with the remaining potatoes.

SERVES 6

LYONNAISE POTATOES

The sweetness of the caramelized onions plays beautifully off the buttery flavor of the potatoes, making this a particularly suitable accompaniment to steak or other hearty cuts of meat and game. This special dish can be easily prepared with ingredients that are common to most households.

6 LARGE IDAHO POTATOES, PEELED AND BOILED

4 TABLESPOONS (½ STICK) SALTED BUTTER

4 CUPS JULIENNED YELLOW ONIONS (ABOUT 3 LARGE ONIONS)

¼ CUP CLARIFIED BUTTER (PAGE 248)

SALT AND FRESHLY GROUND WHITE PEPPER TO TASTE

CHOPPED CURLY PARSLEY, FOR GARNISH

Slice the boiled potatoes in half lengthwise. Turn a quarter turn and slice again to create half rounds.

Melt the salted butter in a large nonstick sauté pan over high heat. Add the onions and sauté for 8 to 10 minutes, until the onions start to caramelize. Deglaze the pan with ¼ cup water to moisten the onions and lift any sugars that are on the bottom of the pan. Toss again and remove the onions to a separate dish. Set aside.

Return the empty pan to high heat. Add the clarified butter and the potatoes and toss the pan to evenly coat the potatoes in butter. Sauté the potatoes for 8 to 10 minutes, until they begin to turn a light golden brown color. Add the caramelized onions and sauté for an additional 3 to 4 minutes to allow the flavors to marry. Season with salt and white pepper. Garnish with chopped parsley and serve hot.

SERVES 6

POTATOES AU GRATIN

When the golden cheese and crumb crust is broken it reveals a silky molten interior.

4 Idaho potatoes, peeled and boiled

2 cups Béchamel Sauce (page 251)

2 cups shredded sharp Cheddar cheese

Salt and freshly ground white pepper to taste

1 cup seasoned dried bread crumbs

¼ cup Parmesan cheese

¼ cup Clarified Butter (page 248)

Preheat the broiler on low.

Coarsely chop the boiled potatoes. To a large sauté pan over medium heat, add the potatoes, béchamel sauce, and Cheddar cheese and simmer until all of the cheese is melted. Stir until the ingredients are incorporated. Season the potatoes with salt and pepper.

Transfer the potato mixture to a 13 × 9 × 2-inch ovenproof baking dish. Smooth out the top of the potatoes to create an even layer. Mix the bread crumbs and Parmesan cheese together in a small bowl and sprinkle the mixture over the potatoes. Drizzle the clarified butter over the bread crumbs and broil the dish for 8 to 10 minutes, until a golden brown crust is formed. Serve immediately.

SERVES 6

THE LONGEST LINE

Galatoire's Restaurant is known for devoted customers. On any given afternoon, you can see them standing in a long line that weaves down Bourbon Street as they await a table. To launch the beginning of Galatoire's one hundredth year in business, the restaurant attempted to attract enough people to form the world's longest line and set a world record. The line formed on the afternoon of Monday, January 10, 2005, outside of the restaurant, and Galatoire's opened its doors from four to seven p.m. to absolutely anyone who wanted to come to the party.

A street celebration featuring live jazz music was held on Bourbon Street, outside of the restaurant, and Galatoire's awarded prizes to random people in line, including dinner for four at the restaurant and an assortment of hundredth-anniversary commemorative pieces. The first 100 people in line were eligible for the grand prize—a reserved table for six on the Friday before Mardi Gras, the busiest day of the year.

Though approximately 2,500 people turned up over the course of three hours and Galatoire's served up 1,500 pounds of Shrimp Rémoulade and poured countless glasses of wine, beer, and champagne, we didn't break the world record.

Galatoire's was simply the site of another great party.

SPINACH ROCKEFELLER

Oysters Rockefeller without the oysters. Spinach Rockefeller, also known as "Rock Spinach" at Galatoire's, can be baked in a large dish, as suggested here, or it can be baked in individual gratin dishes. It is crucial that a maximum of surface space be exposed to the broiler in order to get the desirable light, crackled crust and browned edges on the dish. Do not bake this in a deep casserole dish without adequate surface exposure.

If Herbsaint liqueur is unavailable in your area you may substitute Pernod in the dish.

¾ CUP CHOPPED FENNEL (BULB ONLY)

¼ CUP CHOPPED LEEKS (GREEN AND WHITE PARTS)

¼ CUP FINELY CHOPPED CURLY PARSLEY

¼ CUP FINELY CHOPPED SCALLIONS (GREEN AND WHITE PARTS)

¼ CUP CHOPPED CELERY

¼ CUP KETCHUP

2½ CUPS COOKED AND DRAINED CHOPPED FROZEN SPINACH

½ TEASPOON SALT

½ TEASPOON CAYENNE PEPPER

½ TEASPOON FRESHLY GROUND WHITE PEPPER

1 TEASPOON DRIED THYME LEAVES

1 TEASPOON GROUND ANISE

2 TEASPOONS WORCESTERSHIRE SAUCE

¼ CUP HERBSAINT LIQUEUR

1 CUP (2 STICKS) MELTED SALTED BUTTER

½ CUP SEASONED DRIED BREAD CRUMBS

1 CUP HEAVY WHIPPING CREAM

Preheat the oven to 350°F.

In a food processor combine the fennel, leeks, parsley, scallions, celery, ketchup, spinach, salt, cayenne, white pepper, thyme, anise, Worcestershire, and Herbsaint. Purée the mixture thoroughly. Using a rubber spatula, scrape the contents of the food processor into a large mixing bowl. Add the butter and the bread crumbs and stir in the cream. Ensure that the mixture is well blended.

Transfer the mixture to a 13 × 9 × 2-inch baking dish. Smooth the top so that it is an even layer. Bake for 8 to 10 minutes, until heated through. Once the spinach is heated through, increase the oven temperature to broil. Place the dish under the broiler for 3 to 4 minutes until the top is bubbling and has formed a crust. Serve immediately.

SERVES 6

Desserts and Grand Finales

GALATOIRE'S IS A FAVORITE PLACE for celebrations, and the sight of a crème caramel, bread pudding, or wedge of pie holding aloft a single lighted candle is a common one. And accompanying them are the sounds of Reynard Lavigne's booming baritone or Imre Szalai's heavy Hungarian accent as one or the other leads the staff and restaurant patrons in versions of "Happy birthday to . . ." or "Happy anniversary to . . ." or "Happy whatever to whomever." The public acknowledgment of those celebrations typically coincides with dessert.

In 2003, just after the start of the war in Iraq, New Orleans's *Times-Picayune* columnist Angus Lind wrote of a celebration in honor of Geary Mason, a stockbroker and a major in the Mississippi Army National Guard Special Forces unit. Friends and family put together a birthday party and a good luck "bon voyage" gathering at Galatoire's just before he was to leave for active duty overseas.

"Toward the end of the meal," Lind wrote, "some champagne arrived, drinks were filled and, as happens at Galatoire's, it got crazy."

In celebration of Mason's birthday his waiter presented him with a crème caramel with candles in it, and the waiter tapped a glass to get the other patrons' attention. The customers were then told that the honoree was about to leave to fight overseas and were asked to join in wishing him well and singing "Happy Birthday."

"The crowd obliged, gave him a standing ovation, and afterward, as everyone sat down, Tommy Mason (Mason's brother) started softly singing and humming, almost under his breath, 'God Bless America.' All of a sudden it just picked up steam. It was unbelievable. The whole place was singing 'God Bless America.' Everyone got into it. It was very moving, with tension about Iraq hanging over people's heads. It was a very patriotic moment. It really sent chills down your spine.

"There were some senior ladies dining there that evening. They came over and each gave Mason a kiss. One said her husband fought in World War II.

Another said hers fought in the Korean War. They asked Mason to take a picture with them for their family album. There was a couple from San Diego. They said they had never seen anything like this in their lives."

Lind, a regular patron who has often witnessed the special charms of the restaurant before, closed the article with "Welcome to New Orleans and Galatoire's, folks."

BERRY NAPOLEON WITH GRAND MARNIER SABAYON

New desserts do not come often to Galatoire's menu. But this was a sensational one. Use the freshest berries that are common to your area—either one type of berry or a mixture of several.

1 CUP GRANULATED SUGAR

18 LARGE EGG YOLKS, PLUS 1 LARGE EGG

2 TEASPOONS PURE VANILLA EXTRACT

½ CUP GRAND MARNIER LIQUEUR

1 PUFF PASTRY SHEET, APPROXIMATELY 10 × 10 INCHES
(THAW ACCORDING TO MANUFACTURER'S
INSTRUCTIONS)

3 PINTS SEASONAL BERRIES, SUCH AS STRAWBERRIES,
BLACKBERRIES, OR RASPBERRIES

½ CUP CONFECTIONERS' SUGAR

FRESH MINT SPRIGS, FOR GARNISH

To make the sabayon, place a medium pot with 3 cups of water over high heat to create a double boiler. Combine the granulated sugar and egg yolks in a medium metal mixing bowl and place the bowl over the pot of simmering water so it rests on top of it. Whisk the ingredients continuously for 8 to 10 minutes until stiff peaks form and the volume has doubled. Remove the bowl from atop the pot and whisk in the vanilla and Grand Marnier. Refrigerate the sabayon until cooled.

Preheat the oven to 350°F.

Cut the puff pastry into 6 rectangles, each approximately 3 × 5 inches. Place the rectangles on a cookie sheet lined with parchment paper. Whisk the whole egg and ¼ cup water together in a small bowl to create a wash. Brush the top of the pastry dough with the egg wash. This will help it to brown. Bake for 13 to 15 minutes, until it has risen and turned golden brown. Remove the pan from the oven. Slice the pastries horizontally to create 2 pieces of equal size. One piece will serve as the bottom, the other the top.

Mix the berries in a large bowl. Add the cooled sabayon and toss until the berries are evenly coated.

Place the bottom pieces of pastry at the centers of 6 dessert plates. Evenly distribute the mixture of berries and sabayon atop the puff pastries. Place the caps of the pastry over the berry mixture. Sift confectioners' sugar over the napoleons and garnish with mint sprigs.

SERVES 6

BREAD PUDDING WITH BANANA SAUCE

There was a time when dessert was often overlooked at Galatoire's. Our patrons were prone to eat and drink heartily throughout the savory portions of their meals and seemed to regard our desserts as little more than adequate supports for celebratory candles.

This simple, elegant dish changed all that. Unlike most bread puddings, this one is light and airy, its texture resembling that of pain perdu, *or "French toast."*

If you do not have an oversized muffin pan, one-cup ramekins or baking dishes that have been well buttered may be used to cook the puddings.

---

11 LARGE EGGS

1⅓ CUPS GRANULATED SUGAR

1 QUART WHOLE MILK

1 TEASPOON VANILLA EXTRACT

1 TEASPOON GROUND CINNAMON

TWENTY-FOUR ¾-INCH SLICES OF FRENCH BREAD
(BAGUETTES)

1 POUND SALTED BUTTER

1 POUND LIGHT BROWN SUGAR

4 BANANAS

½ CUP PRALINE LIQUEUR

Preheat the oven to 350°F.

In a large mixing bowl, combine the eggs, granulated sugar, milk, vanilla, and cinnamon and whisk until well blended. In a nonstick oversized muffin pan (for 12) place 2 slices of the bread into the bottom of each muffin cup. Pour the egg and milk mixture into each muffin cup. Allow the bread to absorb the mixture and repeat the process until the bread is saturated and the muffin cup is full (it might take 3 or 4 fillings to totally saturate the bread and fill the cup). Bake the pudding mixture for 35 minutes, or until the pudding has turned golden and set in the pan.

While the pudding is in the oven, melt the butter in a 2-quart saucepan over medium heat. Add the light brown sugar and whisk over the heat until smooth. Slice the bananas, stir them into the sauce, and add the praline liqueur. Reduce the heat to low to keep the sauce warm.

When the pudding is baked, remove from the oven and allow it to sit for 15 minutes to cool. Invert the muffin pan to remove the puddings and expose the custard. Place each on the center of a plate and ladle the sauce onto the pudding. Serve immediately.

SERVES 12

BITTERSWEET CHOCOLATE CHEESECAKE

This dessert is sure to please both children and adults. Plan to prepare the cheesecake the night before you will be serving it. Whip the cream just before presenting the dessert.

---

24 OREO COOKIES

½ CUP (1 STICK) SALTED BUTTER, MELTED

1 POUND CREAM CHEESE, SOFTENED

½ CUP GRANULATED SUGAR

½ TEASPOON PURE VANILLA EXTRACT

2 LARGE EGGS

6 OUNCES BITTERSWEET CHOCOLATE, MELTED

3 CUPS HEAVY WHIPPING CREAM

½ CUP CONFECTIONERS' SUGAR

2 OUNCES SOLID BITTERSWEET CHOCOLATE

Preheat the oven to 350°F.

Crush the Oreo cookies in a food processor until they are reduced to small crumbs. Combine the cookie crumbs and butter in a mixing bowl. Mix thoroughly with a rubber spatula to fully blend the butter and crumbs. Press the mixture onto the bottom and 1 inch up the sides of a 9-inch springform pan. Bake the crust for 8 to 10 minutes, until firm. Remove from the oven and cool the pan on a wire rack. Keep the oven at 350°F.

In a large mixing bowl, beat the cream cheese, granulated sugar, and vanilla until smooth. Stir in the eggs and melted chocolate. Beat until the ingredients are well incorporated, then stir in 1 cup of the whipping cream. Pour the mixture into the cooled crust and bake for 40 to 45 minutes, or until the center is almost set. Remove the cheesecake from the oven, let it cool to room temperature on a wire rack, and refrigerate overnight.

Place the remaining 2 cups of whipping cream into a chilled stainless-steel bowl. Whisk continuously until stiff peaks form. Add the confectioners' sugar and whisk until incorporated.

Slice or grate the solid bittersweet chocolate into shavings.

Slice the cheesecake into 10 even slices. Center each piece on a chilled dessert plate, garnish with a dollop of whipped cream, sprinkle with chocolate shavings.

SERVES 10

CAFÉ BRÛLOT

Flaming, booze-soaked coffee makes a most dramatic end to a meal at Galatoire's. Though our staff members may masterfully swirl and twirl tendrils of this fragrant, flaming liquid as they prepare the dish at tableside, we do not recommend that you do this at home. Just keep it simple. Ladle it into a demitasse cup and enjoy.

---

1 ORANGE

1 LEMON

12 WHOLE CLOVES

3 CINNAMON STICKS

2 OUNCES BRANDY

2 OUNCES ORANGE LIQUEUR, SUCH AS GRAND MARNIER

2 TABLESPOONS SUGAR

6 CUPS BREWED FRENCH-ROAST COFFEE, KEPT HOT

Carefully carve the peel from the orange in a continuous coil fashion. Cut the lemon peel into ¼-inch curls and set aside (see Note). Stud the orange peel with the cloves and spear one end of the coil with a fork. Set aside. Reserve the flesh of the orange and lemon for another use.

In a small saucepan, combine the lemon peel, cinnamon sticks, liquors, and sugar over low heat until very warm to allow the ingredients to marry. The warmth is also required to ignite the *brûlot;* cold liquor will not flame. Once the ingredients are heated, pour them into a *brûlot* bowl or a stainless-steel bowl that has a flat bottom. Ignite the liquor by holding a match to a ladle full of the liquor. Once the ladle is lit, slowly lower it to the liquor in the bowl. Hold the fork with the dangling clove-studded orange coil over the ignited bowl. Take extreme care not to burn yourself. Stir the flaming liquor with the ladle and ladle the liquor over the orange coil you are holding over the bowl. The flame will spiral down the coil of orange peel and cloves, back into the bowl. Once you have poured the flaming liquor down the coil several times to incorporate those flavors, remove the coil from the fork and put it in the bowl. Slowly pour in the coffee while stirring to extinguish the flame. Ladle small amounts of the aromatic coffee mixture into demitasse cups.

SERVES 6

Note: While it will not make as striking a presentation, an option for the home cook is to simply cut the peel from the citrus fruits and remove the pith, instead of cutting the peel into elaborate coils. The pieces of orange peel can then be studded with the cloves.

CARAMEL CUP CUSTARD

This very classic French crème caramel has been a mainstay on Galatoire's dessert menu since the day the restaurant opened.

2½ CUPS SUGAR

1 QUART WHOLE MILK

10 LARGE EGGS

2 TABLESPOONS PURE VANILLA EXTRACT

Preheat the oven to 350°F.

Melt 1 cup of the sugar in a small, heavy saucepan over very low heat, stirring occasionally, for 8 to 10 minutes. When the sugar turns golden brown, slowly stir in ¼ cup water. Cook the caramel sauce for 2 to 3 minutes, stirring, then remove the pan from the heat. Pour enough hot caramel to coat the bottom of each of 12 custard cups. Put the custard cups in a 2-inch-deep baking pan. Fill the pan with water until it is halfway up the sides of the cups. Set aside while making the custard.

Heat the milk in a large pan over medium-high heat until it simmers. In the meantime, combine the remaining 1½ cups of sugar, the eggs, and the vanilla in a separate bowl. Whisk until smooth. Slowly add the milk to the eggs to temper them. Once all of the milk has been incorporated, strain the custard mix through a fine-mesh strainer. Discard any solids.

Fill each of the caramel-coated cups with the liquid custard. Cover the pan with foil and create a seal at the edges.

Bake the custards for 30 minutes. Remove the foil and bake for an additional 30 to 40 minutes. Touch the top of one custard to check for firmness. It should have a lightly springy texture that does not stick to your finger.

Remove the custards from the water bath, let them cool to room temperature, and refrigerate until chilled.

Separate the custards from the sides of the cups using a small paring knife. Invert the cups onto small dessert plates or bowls. Remove the cups to allow the rich caramel to run down the sides of the custards.

SERVES 12

CHOCOLATE PECAN PIE

No southern holiday dinner is complete without a traditional pecan pie. Here we have added semisweet chocolate for extra richness and flavor. If you prefer a traditional pie, simply omit the chocolate. Either version is wonderful served warm or cold, with or without ice cream or whipped cream.

1 ¼ CUPS ALL-PURPOSE FLOUR

¾ TEASPOON SALT

½ CUP VEGETABLE SHORTENING, CHILLED

3 TABLESPOONS ICE WATER

4 LARGE EGGS

¾ CUP SUGAR

1 ½ CUPS LIGHT CORN SYRUP

1 TABLESPOON SALTED BUTTER, MELTED AND COOLED

1 TEASPOON PURE VANILLA EXTRACT

1 CUP PECAN HALVES

½ CUP SEMISWEET CHOCOLATE CHIPS

Whisk the flour and ¼ teaspoon of the salt together in a medium mixing bowl. Using a pastry blender, cut in the shortening until the mixture resembles large crumbs. Drizzle 2 tablespoons of ice water over the flour. Toss the mixture with a fork to moisten and add a few more drops of ice water, one at a time, until the mixture is blended into dough.

Gently gather the pieces of dough to form a disk. Wrap the disk in plastic wrap and refrigerate for at least 30 minutes before rolling.

Prepare the filling for the pie while the dough is in the refrigerator: Beat the eggs lightly and add the sugar, the remaining ½ teaspoon of salt, the corn syrup, butter, and vanilla. Stir until mixed well. Set aside.

Preheat the oven to 400°F.

Roll out the dough and transfer it to a 9-inch pie pan. Cut off any excess and crimp the edges of the dough around the top of the pan.

Spread the pecan halves and chocolate chips in the bottom of the shell. Pour the filling into the shell, covering the pecans and chocolate. Place in the oven and immediately reduce the heat to 350°F. Bake for 40 to 45 minutes, until the mixture is firm in the center and the crust is golden brown. Cool before serving in order to slice. If you like your pie warm, you can reheat the slices in the oven at 200°F–250°F. Be sure to remove the slices from the oven just as they get warm so that the filling does not melt.

SERVES 8

CHOCOLATE DECADENCE WITH RASPBERRY SAUCE

This dessert is proof that even Galatoire's is not entirely immune to trends. Even we were swayed by the immense popularity of flourless chocolate cake. When paired with a fresh raspberry sauce, it is simply irresistible.

3 PINTS FRESH RASPBERRIES

2¼ CUPS SUGAR

1½ CUPS PORT WINE

1 TABLESPOON PURE VANILLA EXTRACT

1 TEASPOON GRATED ORANGE ZEST

14 OUNCES SEMISWEET CHOCOLATE

½ CUP (1 STICK) UNSALTED BUTTER, SOFTENED

7 LARGE EGGS, SEPARATED

PINCH OF SALT

¾ CUP HEAVY WHIPPING CREAM

FRESH MINT SPRIGS, FOR GARNISH

Make the raspberry sauce: Combine the raspberries, 1½ cups of the sugar, the port, vanilla, orange zest, and ½ cup water in a saucepan over medium heat and cook for about 20 minutes, stirring occasionally, until the sauce coats the back of a spoon. Strain the sauce through a fine-mesh strainer into another saucepan over medium heat, using a small ladle to force the juice from the seeds and pulp. Reduce the strained sauce for 15 to 20 minutes, until syrupy. Let the sauce cool to room temperature, then refrigerate while baking the cake.

Preheat the oven to 350°F.

Using a double boiler set over medium-high heat, melt 8 ounces of the semisweet chocolate.

While the chocolate is melting, combine the butter and the remaining ¾ cup of sugar in a mixing bowl and beat by hand until smooth. Add the egg yolks and whisk until incorporated. Slowly drizzle in the melted chocolate and blend until fully incorporated.

In a separate mixing bowl, whisk the egg whites with the salt and beat until soft peaks form. Gently fold the egg whites into the chocolate mixture.

Butter a 9-inch springform pan and line the bottom with a disk of parchment paper. Pour the chocolate batter into the pan and bake for 40 to 45 minutes. Touch the center of the cake to check for doneness. The cake is ready when the center springs back from the touch.

Allow the cake to cool for 5 minutes. Loosen the edges with a knife, then release it from the springform pan and invert onto a wire cooling rack to finish cooling.

While the cake is cooling, make the chocolate ganache: Melt the remaining 6 ounces of semisweet chocolate in a double boiler. Whisk the heavy whipping cream into the chocolate and blend until incorporated. Reduce the heat under the double boiler to low to keep the ganache warm.

Place a jelly-roll pan under the wire cooling rack that is holding the cake. The pan will catch the dripping ganache. Ladle the ganache over the cake and spread evenly using a cake spatula. Allow the cake to sit for 30 minutes so the ganache will set.

Cut the cake into 12 even slices. Ladle the raspberry sauce onto 12 chilled dessert plates and center the cake slices atop each. Garnish with fresh mint. Serve warm.

SERVES 12

C R Ê P E S   M A I S O N

The crêpes for this signature dessert can be made in advance and refrigerated if layered with parchment or wax paper. If they are going to be used immediately, just stack them on a plate. For variation try filling the crêpes with different flavors of jams and jellies.

4 LARGE EGGS	¾ CUP FINE-QUALITY RED CURRANT JELLY
1 CUP WHOLE MILK	1 CUP SLICED ALMONDS, TOASTED
1 TABLESPOON MELTED SALTED BUTTER	6 TEASPOONS GRATED ORANGE ZEST
1 CUP ALL-PURPOSE FLOUR	2 CUPS CONFECTIONERS' SUGAR
PINCH OF SALT	1 CUP GRAND MARNIER LIQUEUR

In a medium mixing bowl, whisk the eggs, milk, melted butter, flour, and salt until smooth. Let the mixture stand for 30 minutes to allow the air bubbles to escape.

Lightly spray a crêpe pan or small nonstick sauté pan with vegetable oil spray. Place the pan over medium heat. Stir the crêpe batter. Pour ¼ cup of the batter into the hot pan and immediately tilt and rotate the pan to coat the entire bottom of the pan. Cook for 1 to 2 minutes, until the edges begin to brown and the batter is set. Loosen the edges of the crêpe with a spatula, then flip it in the pan. Almost immediately, slide the crêpe out of the pan and onto parchment paper. Repeat the process to make at least 12 crêpes in all.

Preheat the broiler on low.

Lay out the crêpes on a flat work space. Put 1 tablespoon of jelly in the center of each. Fold the crêpes in half and roll into the shape of a cigar. Place 2 crêpes in the centers of 6 ovenproof dessert plates and sprinkle equal amounts of toasted almonds atop each. Now sprinkle 1 teaspoon of orange zest atop each plate and sift enough confectioners' sugar atop the crêpes to fully coat all of the almonds and zest.

Place the plates under the broiler. The sugar will caramelize atop the dessert and will protect the almonds and zest from burning under the broiler. Remove from the broiler after 30 to 40 seconds when the desserts begin to brown.

Serve the hot dessert plates atop chargers or other liners. Finish each with a dash of Grand Marnier. Serve at once.

SERVES 6

"*I just* ran into a friend who, still today, talks about that party. She remembers the room, how very long it was and how you could look out of those huge windows and see people strolling down the street. My fondest memories are of the food and of Mr. Bobby, who served us. I can still see all that crabmeat, delicately layered on dish after dish that was delivered to our table."

It is amazing how the years can go by, but the memories remain as clear as yesterday. "You know it was something when people are still talking about it today," a chuckling Clarisse Gooch says, but quickly adds, "Oh, there aren't many of us talking because there are so few of us left. But whenever I see those ladies, we just get to talking about that party."

"That party," as Clarisse fondly refers to it, was her Sweet Sixteen birthday party. The year was 1925 and the host was her favorite uncle, Gabriel Galatoire, affectionately referred to as Uncle Gabie. "You must understand," Clarisse emphasizes, "in those days you didn't have such lavish affairs, especially for a sixteenth birthday party. That was unheard of! But Uncle Gabie turned the second-floor dining room into a dream. He even served me my favorite dessert, half a cantaloupe with vanilla ice cream and a cherry."

Whether it's a Sweet Sixteen or an anniversary, whether the guests talk about it today or fifty years from now, Galatoire's Restaurant is proud to have been making memories with our friends for the past century.

CRÊPES SUZETTE

When prepared tableside at Galatoire's, this internationally famed dish is liberally doused with Grand Marnier liqueur and ignited to flaming glory before it is served. While this makes for a dramatic presentation, it is a bit too risky for the home cook. We have simplified the presentation without losing any of the rich orange and butter flavors for which the dish is known.

The crêpes can be made in advance and refrigerated if layered with parchment or wax paper. If they are going to be used immediately, just stack them on a plate.

---

4 LARGE EGGS

1 CUP WHOLE MILK

1 TABLESPOON MELTED SALTED BUTTER, COOLED

1 CUP ALL-PURPOSE FLOUR

PINCH OF SALT

1 CUP (2 STICKS) SALTED BUTTER

1 CUP SUGAR

½ CUP FRESH ORANGE JUICE

½ CUP GRAND MARNIER LIQUEUR

2 TEASPOONS PURE VANILLA EXTRACT

1 ORANGE, HALVED, EACH HALF CUT INTO 6 HALF
    CIRCLES, AND SEEDED

In a medium mixing bowl, whisk the eggs, milk, melted butter, flour, and salt until smooth. Let the mixture stand for 30 minutes to allow the air bubbles to escape.

Lightly spray a crêpe pan or small nonstick sauté pan with vegetable oil spray. Place the pan over medium heat. Stir the crêpe batter. Pour ¼ cup of the batter into the hot pan and immediately tilt and rotate the pan to coat the entire bottom of the pan. Cook for 1 to 2 minutes, until the edges begin to brown and the batter is set. Loosen the edges of the crêpe with a spatula, then flip it in the pan. Almost immediately, slide the crêpe out of the pan and onto parchment paper. Repeat the process to make at least 12 crêpes in all.

Melt the ½ pound of butter in a medium sauté pan over low heat. Add the sugar and whisk until smooth. Add the orange juice, Grand Marnier, and vanilla and whisk until incorporated. Place the half circles of orange into the sauce. Raise the heat to medium-low and simmer for about 5 minutes, until the oranges are candied and the sauce becomes syrupy and coats the back of a spoon.

Fold each of the crêpes in half and in half again to form a quarter circle. Place all 12 folded crêpes into the pan with the sauce, ensuring that they are fully submerged and evenly coated with the sauce. Simmer for an additional minute.

Center 2 crêpes in each of 6 small dessert plates. Drizzle them with the sauce, garnish each plate with 2 candied oranges, and serve.

SERVES 6

PORT-POACHED PEARS WITH CINNAMON CRÈME ANGLAISE

This dish is just right for holiday entertaining when Anjou pears are at their most sweet and succulent. Look for firm yellow-green fruit with blush-colored spots. Both components of the dish can be made the day before and refrigerated. Simply assemble the dish just prior to serving.

3 CUPS (750 ML) PORT WINE

JUICE OF 1 ORANGE

HALF OF THE RIND OF 1 ORANGE

1 CUP SUGAR

1 CINNAMON STICK, PLUS ADDITIONAL FOR GARNISH

3 FIRM FRESH PEARS, PREFERABLY ANJOU, PEELED, CORED, AND CUT IN HALF LENGTHWISE

1½ CUPS HEAVY WHIPPING CREAM

7 LARGE EGG YOLKS

1 TEASPOON GROUND CINNAMON

1 TEASPOON PURE VANILLA EXTRACT

FRESH MINT, FOR GARNISH

Combine the port, orange juice, orange rind, ⅓ cup of the sugar, and 1 cinnamon stick in a medium saucepan and bring to a boil over high heat. Reduce the heat to medium and simmer for 5 minutes. Add the pears and simmer for 15 additional minutes, or until the pears are fork-tender. Remove the pears with a slotted spoon, drain, and chill. Discard the liquid.

Add the cream to a medium saucepan over low heat. Reduce the heat to very low if it begins to simmer.

While the cream is heating, place a medium pot with 3 cups of water over high heat to create a double boiler. Combine the remaining ⅔ cup of sugar, the egg yolks, ground cinnamon, and vanilla in a medium metal mixing bowl and place the bowl over the pot of boiling water so it rests on top of it. Whisk the ingredients continuously for 15 to 20 minutes, until the mixture doubles in volume and forms very thick ribbons. Slowly pour the hot cream into the egg mixture, whisking constantly. Cook for approximately 10 minutes, until the sauce is thick enough to coat the back of a spoon. Remove the crème anglaise from the double boiler and refrigerate for at least 6 hours, until chilled.

For each dessert, fill the base of an 8-inch plate with crème anglaise. Using a paring knife, slice the pear halves lengthwise beginning 1 inch from the top stem, making a cut every ¼ inch through the bell-shaped bottom. There should be 6 to 8 slices in each half pear. Apply slight pressure with the heel of your hand to the bottom of the pear where the slices are to create a fan.

Place the pear fans in the centers of the plates over the cinnamon crème anglaise. Garnish with additional cinnamon sticks and fresh mint. Serve chilled.

SERVES 6

SWEET POTATO CHEESECAKE

The dense texture of the sweet potato is made rich and creamy with the addition of cream cheese. This texture plays beautifully against the crackle of the graham cracker crust and the surprise of the spicy pecans.

Plan ahead to make this dish the day before you will serve it. All that you'll need to do before serving is make the caramel sauce.

1½ CUPS GRAHAM CRACKER CRUMBS

3 CUPS GRANULATED SUGAR

⅓ CUP SALTED BUTTER, MELTED

THREE 3-OUNCE PACKAGES CREAM CHEESE, SOFTENED

¼ CUP LIGHT BROWN SUGAR

1 LARGE SWEET POTATO (ABOUT 18 OUNCES), PEELED, COOKED, AND MASHED

2 LARGE EGGS

⅔ CUP EVAPORATED WHOLE MILK

2 TABLESPOONS CORNSTARCH

¼ TEASPOON GROUND CINNAMON

⅛ TEASPOON GROUND NUTMEG

2 CUPS SOUR CREAM, AT ROOM TEMPERATURE

1 TEASPOON PURE VANILLA EXTRACT

1 RECIPE SPICY PECANS (PAGE 264)

Preheat the oven to 350°F.

Combine the crumbs, ¼ cup of the granulated sugar, and the butter in a mixing bowl until incorporated. Press onto the bottom and 1 inch up the sides of a 9-inch springform pan. Bake for 6 to 8 minutes. Do not allow to brown. Remove from the oven and cool.

In a large bowl, beat the cream cheese, 1 cup of the granulated sugar, and the brown sugar until smooth. Add the sweet potatoes, eggs, evaporated milk, cornstarch, cinnamon, and nutmeg. Beat well until all ingredients are incorporated. Pour into the crust and bake for 55 to 60 minutes, or until the edge is set.

While the cheesecake is in the oven, combine the sour cream, ¼ cup of the granulated sugar, and the vanilla in a large mixing bowl and whip until smooth. Spread the topping over the warm cheesecake once it is removed from the oven. Return the cheesecake to the oven at 350°F and bake for an additional 5 minutes, or until the top is smooth. Remove the cheesecake from the oven and cool on a wire rack. Loosen the edges with a knife, then remove the sides of the springform pan and chill for several hours or overnight.

Make the caramel just prior to when you will serve the dessert: Melt the remaining 1½ cups granulated sugar in a heavy pan over very low heat, stirring occasionally, for 8 to 10 minutes. When the sugar turns golden brown, slowly stir in ¼ cup water. When the sauce is smooth and thick enough to coat the back of a spoon, remove it from the heat and use immediately.

Slice the cheesecake into 12 pieces. Center each piece on a dessert plate and drizzle caramel sauce on top. Sprinkle spicy pecans over and around each piece. Serve immediately.

SERVES 12

Dressings, Sauces, and Seasoning Blends

THE CREOLES ARE FAMOUS for their flavorful sauces, and the perfect execution of a sauce will always be considered an indispensable part of the art of good cooking.

Sauces, particularly Meunière Butter and Béarnaise Sauce, are a crucial component in many dishes at Galatoire's. Please do not try to lighten the hefty fat content of these sauces by substituting other ingredients for the butter that these recipes require. These classic sauces simply die an unflattering death when they are tampered with in the interest of modern diets.

Here we also offer a selection of fresh dressings to complement Galatoire's extensive array of salads and cold appetizers.

BALSAMIC VINAIGRETTE

Use the highest-quality aged balsamic vinegar available and watch the flavor of this simple dressing improve. This will keep for two weeks in the refrigerator.

¼ CUP CREOLE MUSTARD OR ANY COARSE GRAINY
    BROWN MUSTARD

1 TABLESPOON HONEY

1 TABLESPOON WORCESTERSHIRE SAUCE

½ CUP BALSAMIC VINEGAR

1½ CUPS EXTRA-VIRGIN OLIVE OIL

2 TABLESPOONS CREOLE SEASONING (PAGE 257)

1 TEASPOON FRESH THYME LEAVES

1 TEASPOON FINELY MINCED GARLIC

Combine the mustard, honey, Worcestershire, and vinegar in a large mixing bowl and whisk until all ingredients are incorporated. Add the oil in a slow, steady stream while continuously whisking. Add the Creole Seasoning, thyme, and garlic and whisk again.

MAKES 2 CUPS

CLARIFIED BUTTER

This will keep sealed and refrigerated for up to two weeks.

---

1 POUND SALTED BUTTER

In a saucepan over low heat, melt the butter. Remove the pan from the heat and let the butter stand briefly. Skim the milk solids off the top and discard. Strain the butter to remove the remaining sediment. Reserve in a warm place until ready to use, or refrigerate for later use.

MAKES ABOUT 2 CUPS

HOLLANDAISE SAUCE

This classic smooth, rich, creamy sauce is a mainstay in the Galatoire's kitchen. We use it with abandon to embellish seafood, meat, poultry, eggs, and vegetables. Please note that hollandaise sauce should be used shortly after it is made, as reheating will break up the sauce.

6 LARGE EGG YOLKS

2 TABLESPOONS COLD SALTED BUTTER, CUT INTO SMALL
    PIECES

½ TEASPOON SALT

PINCH OF CAYENNE PEPPER

1 TEASPOON FRESH LEMON JUICE

2 TEASPOONS RED WINE VINEGAR

2 CUPS WARM CLARIFIED BUTTER (PAGE 248)

In a double boiler over medium heat, combine the egg yolks with the cold butter, salt, cayenne pepper, lemon juice, and red wine vinegar. Whisk the ingredients continuously until the mixture has increased in volume and achieved a consistency that coats the whisk. Use a ladle to drizzle the clarified butter into the sauce while whisking slowly. If the sauce appears too thick, add a few drops of cold water to achieve the proper consistency.

MAKES 3 CUPS

BÉARNAISE SAUCE

This buttery sauce hails from the Béarn region (Pyrénées-Atlantique) of France, founder Jean Galatoire's homeland. Dishes of béarnaise are a familiar sight on the tables at Galatoire's. Diners scoop it up with Soufflé Potatoes and Creole Fried Eggplant and slather it on steaks, lamb chops, and seafood.

Life is simply too short to live without béarnaise sauce.

¼ CUP TARRAGON-FLAVORED VINEGAR

2 TABLESPOONS DRIED TARRAGON LEAVES

1 TABLESPOON FINELY CHOPPED SCALLIONS (GREEN PARTS ONLY)

1 TEASPOON CHOPPED CURLY PARSLEY

1 RECIPE HOLLANDAISE SAUCE (PAGE 249)

Place the vinegar, tarragon leaves, scallions, and parsley in a small pan over medium heat. Cook for 5 minutes, or until all of the liquid has cooked out of the pan, leaving the tarragon leaves, scallions, and parsley still moist. Set aside while you make the hollandaise sauce.

When the hollandaise sauce is complete, whisk in the tarragon reduction.

MAKES 3 CUPS

BÉCHAMEL SAUCE

This recipe will yield a very thick version of the classic white sauce that serves as a base or additive for numerous French recipes. It is imperative to watch the roux carefully upon adding the flour. It will darken quickly. A blond roux is the desired result here. This béchamel will keep for one week in the refrigerator.

2 CUPS WHOLE MILK

1 CUP (2 STICKS) SALTED BUTTER

½ CUP ALL-PURPOSE FLOUR

In a medium saucepan, heat the milk until simmering. In a medium sauté pan, melt the butter and slowly incorporate the flour, whisking constantly over low heat to make a blond roux. Slowly incorporate 1 cup of the heated milk into the roux, whisking constantly. Cook over low heat for 10 minutes, until the mixture becomes paste-like in consistency. Slowly incorporate the remaining milk and whisk until smooth.

MAKES 2½ CUPS

Galatoire's

CHAMPAGNE AND CAPER BEURRE BLANC

Serve this pungent sauce with mildly flavored meats, poultry, and seafood. We particularly like it with Sautéed Sweetbread Medallions (page 58).

Please note that this should be used the same day it is made.

---

1 CUP CHAMPAGNE OR SPARKLING WINE

JUICE OF 1 LEMON (ABOUT 2 TABLESPOONS)

1 TABLESPOON BLACK PEPPERCORNS

1 TABLESPOON CHOPPED SHALLOTS

1 TABLESPOON CHOPPED GARLIC

1 POUND SALTED BUTTER, CUT INTO PIECES

3 TABLESPOONS NONPAREIL CAPERS, DRAINED

To a small saucepan set over medium heat add the champagne, lemon juice, peppercorns, shallots, and garlic. Simmer for 5 minutes, or until reduced by one third. Whisking constantly, add the butter to the liquid one piece at a time until it has all been incorporated into the sauce. Remove the sauce from the heat and strain through a fine-mesh strainer into a fresh saucepan. Discard the solids. Add the capers to the strained sauce.

MAKES 3 CUPS

Blue Cheese Dressing

This pungent dressing is best made a day in advance, which allows the flavor of the onions to mellow and become sweeter. It will keep, refrigerated, for one week.

1 POUND BLUE CHEESE, MINCED

1 MEDIUM ONION, CHOPPED (ABOUT 1 CUP)

2 TABLESPOONS RED WINE VINEGAR

1 TEASPOON WORCESTERSHIRE SAUCE

½ CUP HALF-AND-HALF

1 RECIPE HOMEMADE MAYONNAISE (PAGE 259)

Place the blue cheese, onions, vinegar, and Worcestershire in a food processor and pulse until smooth. Use a rubber spatula to scrape down the sides of the bowl and pulse again. Remove to a large mixing bowl and whisk in the half-and-half and the mayonnaise.

MAKES 4 CUPS

Cocktail Sauce

This popular condiment complements all manner of chilled and fried seafood. It will keep, refrigerated, for two weeks.

3 CUPS KETCHUP

3 TABLESPOONS WORCESTERSHIRE SAUCE

3 TABLESPOONS PREPARED HORSERADISH

1 TEASPOON TABASCO SAUCE

Combine all ingredients in a large mixing bowl and whisk until incorporated.

MAKES ABOUT 3 CUPS

CRAWFISH BEURRE BLANC

Use only fresh crawfish tails for this sauce. Frozen tails will impart an undesirable gray hue. This sauce should be used the same day it is made. It is delicious with any sautéed or grilled fish or fried seafood.

1 POUND FRESH, PEELED LOUISIANA CRAWFISH TAILS

1 CUP WHITE WINE

JUICE OF 1 LEMON (ABOUT 2 TABLESPOONS)

1 TABLESPOON BLACK PEPPERCORNS

1 TABLESPOON CHOPPED SHALLOTS

1 TABLESPOON CHOPPED FRESH GARLIC

1 POUND SALTED BUTTER, CUT INTO ½-INCH PIECES

In a medium pan over medium heat, sauté half of the crawfish tails. When the crawfish tails and fat begin to brown in the pan, add the white wine, lemon juice, peppercorns, shallots, and garlic. Simmer for 5 minutes, or until reduced by one third. Whisking constantly, add the butter to the liquid one piece at a time until it has all been incorporated into the sauce. Remove the sauce from the heat.

Add the remaining crawfish tails to another pan over medium heat and cook for 2 to 3 minutes, until heated through. Strain the sauce into the pan with the warmed crawfish tails and discard the strained solids, including the original crawfish tails.

MAKES 3 CUPS

CREAMY ROASTED GARLIC VINAIGRETTE

This will keep, chilled in a sealed container, for about one week.

---

1 CUP EXTRA-VIRGIN OLIVE OIL

6 GARLIC CLOVES, PEELED

¼ CUP RICE VINEGAR

1 LARGE EGG YOLK

1 TABLESPOON DIJON MUSTARD

SALT AND FRESHLY GROUND WHITE PEPPER TO TASTE

In a small saucepan over low heat, combine the olive oil and garlic. Make sure the garlic cloves are fully submerged. Cook for 8 to 10 minutes, until the cloves are soft and begin to turn a light caramel color. Remove the oil from the heat and allow it to cool to room temperature to be used later in the dressing.

When the garlic and oil have cooled, in a separate bowl combine the rice vinegar, egg yolk, and Dijon mustard and whisk until blended. Remove the garlic cloves from the oil and add the oil to the egg-yolk mixture in a thin, steady stream, whisking continuously to create an emulsion. Chop all of the soft garlic cloves and mash them into a paste. Whisk the garlic paste into the dressing. Chill the dressing until ready to serve.

MAKES ABOUT 1½ CUPS

CREOLE SAUCE

This sauce will keep for one week in the refrigerator or up to one month in the freezer.

4 LARGE TOMATOES

2 TABLESPOONS SALTED BUTTER

½ CUP CHOPPED CELERY (ABOUT 1 STALK)

1 CUP DICED GREEN BELL PEPPER (ABOUT 1 SMALL)

1½ CUPS DICED YELLOW ONION (ABOUT 1 LARGE)

¼ CUP TOMATO PASTE

1 BAY LEAF

2 TEASPOONS SALT

½ TEASPOON CAYENNE PEPPER, OR TO TASTE

1 TEASPOON HOT PAPRIKA

4 CUPS CHICKEN STOCK

Bring 1 quart of water to a boil in a medium saucepan. Blanch the tomatoes in the water for about 1 minute, just until the skin breaks. Remove the hot tomatoes from the water, drain, and allow them to cool for 10 minutes. Pull off the skin and discard it. Seed and dice the tomatoes, then set them aside.

Melt the butter in a large pot over high heat. Add the celery, bell peppers, onions, and tomatoes and sauté for 7 to 10 minutes, until the tomatoes are nearly dissolved and the vegetables begin to caramelize. Reduce the heat to medium and add the tomato paste, bay leaf, salt, cayenne pepper, and paprika. Allow the mixture to simmer for an additional 3 to 4 minutes, until the vegetables are a rich caramel color. Stir in the stock and reduce the mixture at a low rolling boil over medium heat for 30 minutes. Remove the bay leaf.

MAKES 4 CUPS

CREOLE SEASONING

Every New Orleans cook has some variety of this seasoning blend on hand, either prepackaged or blended to specification, as we suggest here. This will keep, sealed in an airtight container, for about three months.

1 CUP SPANISH HOT PAPRIKA

⅓ CUP SALT

¼ CUP CAYENNE PEPPER

¼ CUP FRESHLY GROUND BLACK PEPPER

3 TABLESPOONS DRIED THYME

3 TABLESPOONS DRIED OREGANO

2 TABLESPOONS GARLIC POWDER

2 TABLESPOONS ONION POWDER

Mix all ingredients thoroughly in a large mixing bowl and store in an airtight container or sealed plastic storage bag. Use as needed. It will keep for 3 months.

MAKES ABOUT 2 CUPS

CREOLE MUSTARD VINAIGRETTE

This bracing, tangy dressing is delicious with fresh tomatoes, preferably Creoles. When pairing it with lettuce we recommend classic iceberg; other lettuces simply wither against the high vinegar content in the dressing.

Do not serve this dressing with bitter varieties of lettuce, such as watercress. The effect will be overpowering. This vinaigrette will keep, refrigerated, for two weeks.

⅓ CUP RED WINE VINEGAR

½ CUP CREOLE MUSTARD OR ANY COARSE, GRAINY
   BROWN MUSTARD

SALT AND FRESHLY GROUND BLACK PEPPER TO TASTE

⅔ CUP VEGETABLE OIL

In a small bowl, combine the vinegar and mustard, and season with salt and pepper. Add the oil in a slow drizzle while whisking to incorporate and create an emulsion.

MAKES 1½ CUPS

Homemade Mayonnaise

Homemade mayonnaise makes such a difference in the final product, and it takes only a few minutes to prepare with ingredients most of us have on hand.

   It will keep in the refrigerator for one week.

---

2 LARGE EGG YOLKS

1 TABLESPOON DIJON MUSTARD

1 TABLESPOON FRESH LEMON JUICE

1 TABLESPOON CHAMPAGNE VINEGAR

1½ CUPS VEGETABLE OIL

SALT AND FRESHLY GROUND WHITE PEPPER TO TASTE

In a medium mixing bowl, whisk the egg yolks, Dijon mustard, lemon juice, and vinegar until they are incorporated. Slowly pour in the vegetable oil in a thin, steady stream while continuously whisking until the mixture has emulsified and thickened. If the mayonnaise gets too thick before all of the oil has been incorporated, whisk in a tablespoon of room-temperature water, and then resume adding the oil. Season with salt and white pepper.

MAKES ABOUT 1½ CUPS

MARCHAND DE VIN

Jean Galatoire would have looked upon this sauce as a classic Bordelaise, the modern New Orleans version of which is simply copious amounts of fresh chopped garlic cooked in butter. In true New Orleans fashion, over the years things became a bit jumbled and this sauce, which really is a version of classic Bordelaise, is instead referred to by locals as Marchand de Vin, *which means "wine merchant [sauce]." It is unclear how this misconception evolved.*

The sauce can be prepared several hours in advance and reheated just prior to serving. It will keep in the refrigerator for one week.

---

3 TABLESPOONS SALTED BUTTER

1½ CUPS SLICED BUTTON MUSHROOMS

SALT AND FRESHLY GROUND BLACK PEPPER TO TASTE

¼ CUP FINELY DICED HAM (ABOUT 1 OUNCE)

¼ CUP THINLY SLICED SCALLIONS (GREEN AND WHITE PARTS)

1 TABLESPOON ALL-PURPOSE FLOUR

1 CUP RED WINE

3 CUPS VEAL DEMI-GLACE (PAGE 267)

Melt the butter in a medium sauté pan over high heat. Add the mushrooms and sauté for 3 minutes, or until tender. Season the mushrooms with salt and pepper and add the ham, scallions, and flour; sauté for an additional 3 minutes, or until the ingredients start to brown. Deglaze the pan with the red wine and simmer for 6 to 8 minutes, until the volume of the liquid is reduced by half. Add the demi-glace, bring the mixture to a boil, and reduce the heat to medium. Allow the sauce to cook at a low rolling boil for 20 minutes, stirring occasionally, until it has a thick, rich consistency that coats the back of a spoon.

MAKES 2 CUPS

MEUNIÈRE BUTTER

What we refer to at Galatoire's as a "meunière butter" is really a beurre noir *("black butter") or* beurre noisette *("nut-brown butter"), and we use it by the gallon. Classic meunière sauce is made in individual portions and incorporates the browned bits from the bottom of the pan after cooking a floured item in butter. The pan is then deglazed with fresh lemon juice. At Galatoire's there is simply no way we could keep up with the demand for the sauce by making individual portions, so we prepare large quantities of the sauce just prior to lunch and dinner each day. It will keep, refrigerated, for two weeks.*

This sauce offers a fine finishing touch for all varieties of fish and shellfish.

1 POUND SALTED BUTTER

1 TABLESPOON FRESH LEMON JUICE

1 TABLESPOON RED WINE VINEGAR

In a medium saucepan over medium heat, melt the butter, whisking constantly, for 8 to 10 minutes, until the sediment in the butter turns dark brown, almost (but not quite) to the point of burning, and the liquid is a deep golden color. Remove the pan from the heat and continue to whisk slowly, adding the lemon juice and the vinegar to the browned butter. The sauce will froth until the acids have evaporated. When the frothing subsides, the sauce is complete.

MAKES 2 CUPS

Spicy Pecans

These pecans make a flavorful, crunchy garnish for salads and offer a lively contrast to the sweetness of our Sweet Potato Cheesecake (page 244). They are also good when eaten by the handful.

These nuts will be best when used within one day of baking but can be kept in an airtight container for up to one month.

---

1 CUP LARGE PECAN HALVES

2 TABLESPOONS SALTED BUTTER

1/2 TEASPOON SALT

1/2 TEASPOON CAYENNE PEPPER

1/2 TEASPOON SUGAR

Preheat the oven to 350°F.

Place the pecan halves in a small baking dish and toast for 6 to 8 minutes, until they turn dark brown. Remove the pan from the oven, add the butter, and toss until all of the nuts are evenly coated. Sprinkle the nuts with the salt, cayenne, and sugar and toss to coat. Spread the nuts in a single layer on a cookie sheet and allow them to cool thoroughly so the seasoning will set.

MAKES 1 CUP

TARTAR SAUCE

Tartar sauce is traditionally served with fried seafood, but some also enjoy it with steamed vegetables or crudités. The sauce will keep, covered and refrigerated, for up to one week.

2 LARGE EGG YOLKS	1½ CUPS VEGETABLE OIL
1 TABLESPOON DIJON MUSTARD	2 TABLESPOONS DILL PICKLE RELISH
1 TABLESPOON FRESH LEMON JUICE	2 TABLESPOONS PETITE NONPAREIL CAPERS, DRAINED
1 TABLESPOON CHAMPAGNE VINEGAR	SALT AND FRESHLY GROUND WHITE PEPPER TO TASTE

In a medium mixing bowl, whisk the egg yolks, mustard, lemon juice, and vinegar until they are incorporated. Slowly pour the vegetable oil into the mixture in a thin, steady stream while continuously whisking until a mayonnaise is created. If the mayonnaise gets too thick before all of the oil has been incorporated, whisk in a tablespoon of room-temperature water, then resume with the oil.

Fold in the relish and capers. Season with salt and white pepper. Chill until needed.

MAKES 1½ CUPS

THYME BEURRE BLANC

This delicately flavored beurre blanc pairs particularly well with fish, chicken, and medallions of veal and pork. As with all the beurre blanc sauces, it should be used the same day you make it.

---

1 CUP DRY WHITE WINE

JUICE OF 1 LEMON (ABOUT 2 TABLESPOONS)

1 TABLESPOON CHOPPED SHALLOTS

1 TABLESPOON CHOPPED GARLIC

1 TEASPOON BLACK PEPPERCORNS

3 SPRIGS OF FRESH THYME

1 POUND SALTED BUTTER, CUT INTO PIECES

Add the wine, lemon juice, shallots, garlic, peppercorns, and thyme to a small saucepan set over medium heat. Simmer for 5 minutes, or until reduced by one third. Whisking constantly, add the butter to the liquid one piece at a time until it has all been incorporated into the sauce. Remove the sauce from the heat and strain through a fine-mesh strainer. Discard the solids.

MAKES 2 CUPS

VEAL DEMI-GLACE

The intense flavor of this rich brown sauce is the foundation for many other sauces. It is slowly cooked for twelve to fourteen hours until it has reduced by half and is the consistency of a thick glaze. The demi-glace can be stored in a sealed jar and will keep, refrigerated, for one week. If frozen it will keep for two months.

---

10 POUNDS VEAL MARROW BONES (HAVE YOUR BUTCHER CUT THEM AS SMALL AS POSSIBLE)

¼ CUP VEGETABLE OIL

2 CARROTS, COARSELY CHOPPED

2 CELERY STALKS, COARSELY CHOPPED

2 RIPE TOMATOES, COARSELY CHOPPED

1 LARGE YELLOW ONION, COARSELY CHOPPED

2 TABLESPOONS TOMATO PASTE

LEAVES FROM 2 SPRIGS OF FRESH THYME

2 BAY LEAVES

12 WHOLE BLACK PEPPERCORNS

1 CUP RED WINE

Preheat the oven to 450°F. In a heavy roasting pan, roast the marrow bones for approximately 30 minutes, turning occasionally, until they are a deep mahogany color.

When the bones are nearly finished, heat the oil in a large stockpot. Add the carrots, celery, tomatoes, and onions and sauté over medium-high heat for 7 to 8 minutes to caramelize the vegetables. When the moisture has cooked out and the vegetables are a rich brown color, add the tomato paste, thyme, bay leaves, and peppercorns and simmer for 1 minute. Place the bones in the stockpot with the vegetables, then add 10 cups of water to cover the ingredients. Use the wine to deglaze the roasting pan, scraping the bits from the bottom of the pan. Add this to the stockpot.

Raise the heat to high, bring the stock to a vigorous boil, and skim the foam from the surface. Reduce the heat to very low and simmer for approximately 12 hours, skimming the surface as necessary. At this stage, you will have a veal stock that can be used in a variety of recipes, such as Turtle Soup au Sherry (page 113).

For the demi-glace, strain the stock and discard the solids. Return the stock to the pot and cook for 1½ to 2 hours over medium-high heat, until reduced by half. Skim the foam from the surface. When the sauce is smooth and gelatinous, remove it from the heat and transfer it to a heat-proof dish. Remove the fat from the top of the demi-glace.

MAKES 1 QUART

Sources

DARTAGNAN: Wild mushrooms, duck, quail, and rabbit
(800) 327-8246
www.dartagnan.com

DEAN & DELUCA: Spices
(800) 221-7714
www.deandeluca.com

HARLON'S LA FISH: Gulf fish and shellfish
(504) 467-3809

HUDSON VALLEY FOIE GRAS: Foie gras
(845) 292-2500
www.hudsonvalleyfoiegras.com

MARCIANTE'S GOURMET SAUSAGE: Andouille sausage and tasso
(504) 279-6760

NATCO: Sweetbreads and cut meat
(504) 525-7224

NEW ORLEANS FISH HOUSE: Gulf fish and shellfish
(504) 821-9700
www.nofishhouse.com

PONCHARTRAIN BLUE: Soft-shell crabs, crabmeat, and gumbo crabs
(504) 220-6666
William_Lawrence@bellsouth.net

Index

Page numbers in italics indicate photographs.